PROBLEM SOLVED!

THE ULTIMATE MEAL PLANNER AND COOKBOOK

@ JOURNALS AND NOTEBOOKS

@ Journals & Notebooks

Meal Planner

	Breakfast	Lunch	Dinner
Monday			
Tuesday			
Wednesday			
Thursaday			
Friday			
Saturday			
Sunday			

thinkpositive ● exercise daily
eat healthy ● dance more
Love often ● be happy

Eat Healthy

Meal Planner

	Breakfast	Lunch	Dinner
Monday			
Tuesday			
Wednesday			
Thursaday			
Friday			
Saturday			
Sunday			

think positive ● exercise daily
eat healthy ● dance more
Love often ● be happy

Eat Healthy

Meal Planner

	Breakfast	Lunch	Dinner
Monday			
Tuesday			
Wednesday			
Thursaday			
Friday			
Saturday			
Sunday			

thinkpositive ● exercise daily
eat healthy ● dance more
Love often ● be happy

Eat Healthy

Meal Planner

	Breakfast	Lunch	Dinner
Monday			
Tuesday			
Wednesday			
Thursaday			
Friday			
Saturday			
Sunday			

thinkpositive ● exercise daily
eat healthy ● dance more
Love often ● be happy

Meal Planner

	Breakfast	Lunch	Dinner
Monday			
Tuesday			
Wednesday			
Thursaday			
Friday			
Saturday			
Sunday			

thinkpositive ● exercise daily
eat healthy ● dance more
Love often ● be happy

Eat Healthy

Meal Planner

	Breakfast	Lunch	Dinner
Monday			
Tuesday			
Wednesday			
Thursaday			
Friday			
Saturday			
Sunday			

thinkpositive ● exercise daily
eat healthy ● dance more
Love often ● be happy

Meal Planner

	Breakfast	Lunch	Dinner
Monday			
Tuesday			
Wednesday			
Thursaday			
Friday			
Saturday			
Sunday			

thinkpositive ● exercise daily
eat healthy ● dance more
Love often ● be happy

Eat Healthy

Meal Planner

	Breakfast	Lunch	Dinner
Monday			
Tuesday			
Wednesday			
Thursaday			
Friday			
Saturday			
Sunday			

thinkpositive ● exercise daily
eat healthy ● dance more
Love often ● be happy

Meal Planner

	Breakfast	Lunch	Dinner
Monday			
Tuesday			
Wednesday			
Thursaday			
Friday			
Saturday			
Sunday			

thinkpositive ● exercise daily
eat healthy ● dance more
Love often ● be happy

Meal Planner

	Breakfast	Lunch	Dinner
Monday			
Tuesday			
Wednesday			
Thursaday			
Friday			
Saturday			
Sunday			

thinkpositive ● exercise daily
eat healthy ● dance more
Love often ● be happy

eat Healthy

Meal Planner

	Breakfast	Lunch	Dinner
Monday			
Tuesday			
Wednesday			
Thursaday			
Friday			
Saturday			
Sunday			

thinkpositive ● exercise daily
eat healthy ● dance more
Love often ● be happy

Eat Healthy

Meal Planner

	Breakfast	Lunch	Dinner
Monday			
Tuesday			
Wednesday			
Thursaday			
Friday			
Saturday			
Sunday			

thinkpositive ● exercise daily
eat healthy ● dance more
Love often ● be happy

Eat Healthy

Meal Planner

	Breakfast	Lunch	Dinner
Monday			
Tuesday			
Wednesday			
Thursaday			
Friday			
Saturday			
Sunday			

thinkpositive ● exercise daily
eat healthy ● dance more
Love often ● be happy

Meal Planner

	Breakfast	Lunch	Dinner
Monday			
Tuesday			
Wednesday			
Thursaday			
Friday			
Saturday			
Sunday			

thinkpositive ● exercise daily
eat healthy ● dance more
Love often ● be happy

Meal Planner

	Breakfast	Lunch	Dinner
Monday			
Tuesday			
Wednesday			
Thursaday			
Friday			
Saturday			
Sunday			

Meal Planner

	Breakfast	Lunch	Dinner
Monday			
Tuesday			
Wednesday			
Thursaday			
Friday			
Saturday			
Sunday			

Meal Planner

	Breakfast	Lunch	Dinner
Monday			
Tuesday			
Wednesday			
Thursaday			
Friday			
Saturday			
Sunday			

thinkpositive ● exercise daily
eat healthy ● dance more
Love often ● be happy

Meal Planner

	Breakfast	Lunch	Dinner
Monday			
Tuesday			
Wednesday			
Thursaday			
Friday			
Saturday			
Sunday			

thinkpositive ● exercise daily
eat healthy ● dance more
Love often ● be happy

Meal Planner

	Breakfast	Lunch	Dinner
Monday			
Tuesday			
Wednesday			
Thursaday			
Friday			
Saturday			
Sunday			

thinkpositive ● exercise daily
eat healthy ● dance more
Love often ● be happy

Eat Healthy

Meal Planner

	Breakfast	Lunch	Dinner
Monday			
Tuesday			
Wednesday			
Thursaday			
Friday			
Saturday			
Sunday			

thinkpositive ● exercise daily
eat healthy ● dance more
Love often ● be happy

Eat Healthy

Meal Planner

	Breakfast	Lunch	Dinner
Monday			
Tuesday			
Wednesday			
Thursaday			
Friday			
Saturday			
Sunday			

thinkpositive ● exercise daily
eat healthy ● dance more
Love often ● be happy

Eat Healthy

Meal Planner

	Breakfast	Lunch	Dinner
Monday			
Tuesday			
Wednesday			
Thursaday			
Friday			
Saturday			
Sunday			

thinkpositive ● exercise daily
eat healthy ● dance more
Love often ● be happy

Meal Planner

	Breakfast	Lunch	Dinner
Monday			
Tuesday			
Wednesday			
Thursaday			
Friday			
Saturday			
Sunday			

thinkpositive ● exercise daily
eat healthy ● dance more
Love often ● be happy

Meal Planner

	Breakfast	Lunch	Dinner
Monday			
Tuesday			
Wednesday			
Thursaday			
Friday			
Saturday			
Sunday			

thinkpositive ● exercise daily
eat healthy ● dance more
Love often ● be happy

Meal Planner

	Breakfast	Lunch	Dinner
Monday			
Tuesday			
Wednesday			
Thursaday			
Friday			
Saturday			
Sunday			

Meal Planner

	Breakfast	Lunch	Dinner
Monday			
Tuesday			
Wednesday			
Thursaday			
Friday			
Saturday			
Sunday			

thinkpositive ● exercise daily
eat healthy ● dance more
Love often ● be happy

Eat Healthy

Meal Planner

	Breakfast	Lunch	Dinner
Monday			
Tuesday			
Wednesday			
Thursaday			
Friday			
Saturday			
Sunday			

thinkpositive ● exercise daily
eat healthy ● dance more
Love often ● be happy

Eat Healthy

Meal Planner

	Breakfast	Lunch	Dinner
Monday			
Tuesday			
Wednesday			
Thursaday			
Friday			
Saturday			
Sunday			

Meal Planner

	Breakfast	Lunch	Dinner
Monday			
Tuesday			
Wednesday			
Thursaday			
Friday			
Saturday			
Sunday			

thinkpositive ● exercise daily
eat healthy ● dance more
Love often ● be happy

Eat Healthy

Meal Planner

	Breakfast	Lunch	Dinner
Monday			
Tuesday			
Wednesday			
Thursaday			
Friday			
Saturday			
Sunday			

thinkpositive ● exercise daily
eat healthy ● dance more
Love often ● be happy

Meal Planner

	Breakfast	Lunch	Dinner
Monday			
Tuesday			
Wednesday			
Thursaday			
Friday			
Saturday			
Sunday			

thinkpositive ● exercise daily
eat healthy ● dance more
Love often ● be happy

Meal Planner

	Breakfast	Lunch	Dinner
Monday			
Tuesday			
Wednesday			
Thursaday			
Friday			
Saturday			
Sunday			

thinkpositive ● exercise daily
eat healthy ● dance more
Love often ● be happy

Eat Healthy

Meal Planner

	Breakfast	Lunch	Dinner
Monday			
Tuesday			
Wednesday			
Thursaday			
Friday			
Saturday			
Sunday			

thinkpositive ● exercise daily
eat healthy ● dance more
Love often ● be happy

Meal Planner

	Breakfast	Lunch	Dinner
Monday			
Tuesday			
Wednesday			
Thursaday			
Friday			
Saturday			
Sunday			

thinkpositive ● exercise daily
eat healthy ● dance more
Love often ● be happy

Meal Planner

	Breakfast	Lunch	Dinner
Monday			
Tuesday			
Wednesday			
Thursaday			
Friday			
Saturday			
Sunday			

thinkpositive ● exercise daily
eat healthy ● dance more
Love often ● be happy

Meal Planner

	Breakfast	Lunch	Dinner
Monday			
Tuesday			
Wednesday			
Thursaday			
Friday			
Saturday			
Sunday			

thinkpositive ● exercise daily
eat healthy ● dance more
Love often ● be happy

Eat Healthy

Meal Planner

	Breakfast	Lunch	Dinner
Monday			
Tuesday			
Wednesday			
Thursaday			
Friday			
Saturday			
Sunday			

thinkpositive ● exercise daily
eat healthy ● dance more
Love often ● be happy

Eat Healthy

Meal Planner

	Breakfast	Lunch	Dinner
Monday			
Tuesday			
Wednesday			
Thursaday			
Friday			
Saturday			
Sunday			

Meal Planner

	Breakfast	Lunch	Dinner
Monday			
Tuesday			
Wednesday			
Thursaday			
Friday			
Saturday			
Sunday			

think positive ● exercise daily
eat healthy ● dance more
Love often ● be happy

Meal Planner

	Breakfast	Lunch	Dinner
Monday			
Tuesday			
Wednesday			
Thursaday			
Friday			
Saturday			
Sunday			

thinkpositive ● exercise daily
eat healthy ● dance more
Love often ● be happy

Eat Healthy

Meal Planner

	Breakfast	Lunch	Dinner
Monday			
Tuesday			
Wednesday			
Thursaday			
Friday			
Saturday			
Sunday			

thinkpositive ● exercise daily
eat healthy ● dance more
Love often ● be happy

Eat Healthy

Meal Planner

	Breakfast	Lunch	Dinner
Monday			
Tuesday			
Wednesday			
Thursaday			
Friday			
Saturday			
Sunday			

Meal Planner

	Breakfast	Lunch	Dinner
Monday			
Tuesday			
Wednesday			
Thursaday			
Friday			
Saturday			
Sunday			

thinkpositive ● exercise daily
eat healthy ● dance more
Love often ● be happy

Meal Planner

	Breakfast	Lunch	Dinner
Monday			
Tuesday			
Wednesday			
Thursaday			
Friday			
Saturday			
Sunday			

thinkpositive ● exercise daily
eat healthy ● dance more
Love often ● be happy

Meal Planner

	Breakfast	Lunch	Dinner
Monday			
Tuesday			
Wednesday			
Thursaday			
Friday			
Saturday			
Sunday			

thinkpositive ● exercise daily
eat healthy ● dance more
Love often ● be happy

Eat Healthy

Meal Planner

	Breakfast	Lunch	Dinner
Monday			
Tuesday			
Wednesday			
Thursaday			
Friday			
Saturday			
Sunday			

thinkpositive ● exercise daily
eat healthy ● dance more
Love often ● be happy

Meal Planner

	Breakfast	Lunch	Dinner
Monday			
Tuesday			
Wednesday			
Thursaday			
Friday			
Saturday			
Sunday			

thinkpositive ● exercise daily
eat healthy ● dance more
Love often ● be happy

Meal Planner

	Breakfast	Lunch	Dinner
Monday			
Tuesday			
Wednesday			
Thursaday			
Friday			
Saturday			
Sunday			

thinkpositive ● exercise daily
eat healthy ● dance more
Love often ● be happy

Meal Planner

	Breakfast	Lunch	Dinner
Monday			
Tuesday			
Wednesday			
Thursaday			
Friday			
Saturday			
Sunday			

thinkpositive ● exercise daily
eat healthy ● dance more
Love often ● be happy

Eat Healthy

Meal Planner

	Breakfast	Lunch	Dinner
Monday			
Tuesday			
Wednesday			
Thursaday			
Friday			
Saturday			
Sunday			

thinkpositive ● exercise daily
eat healthy ● dance more
Love often ● be happy

Eat Healthy

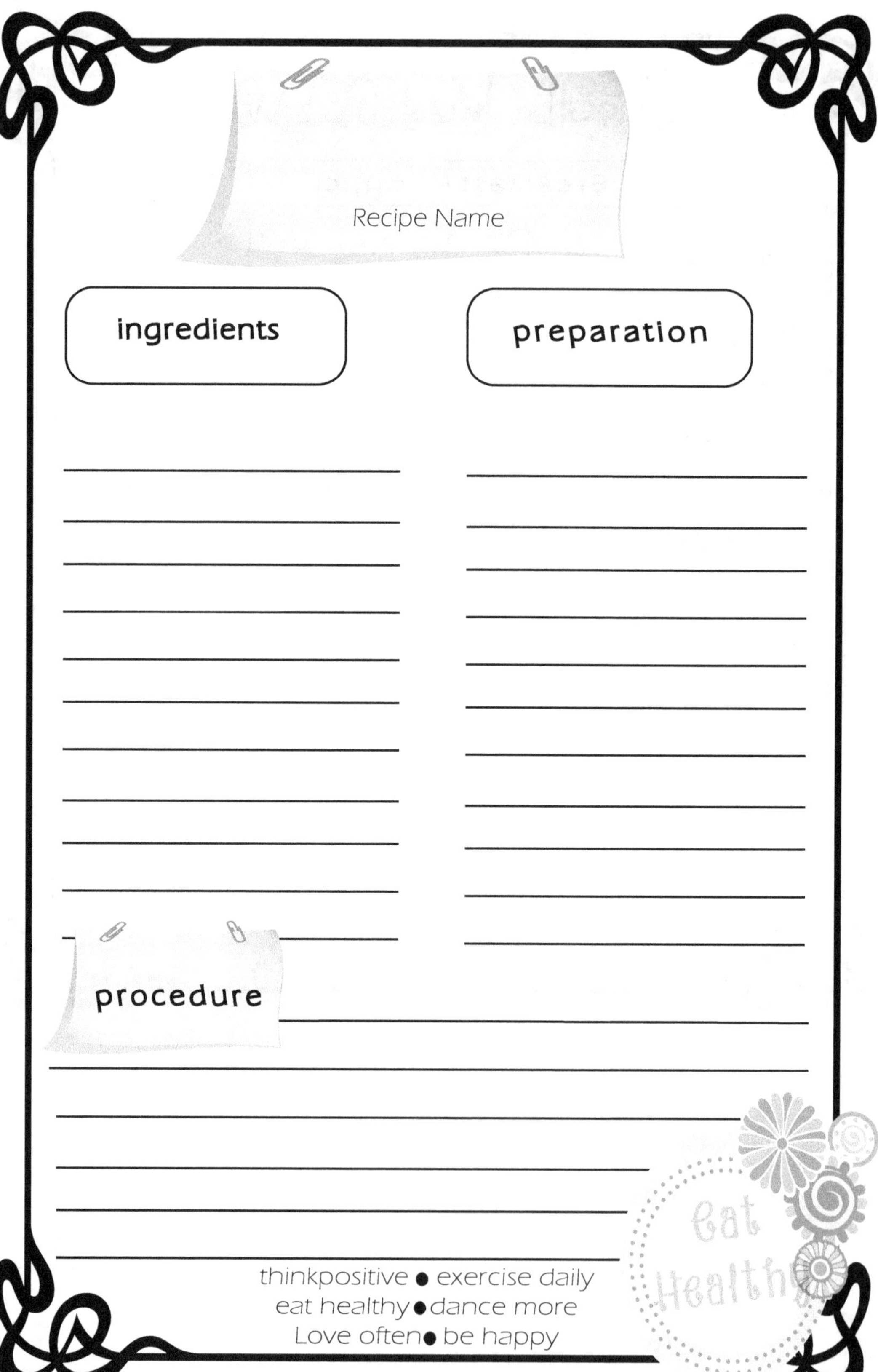

Recipe Name

ingredients

preparation

procedure

Recipe Name
ingredients
preparation
procedure
thinkpositive ● exercise daily
eat healthy ● dance more
Love often ● be happy
eat Healthy

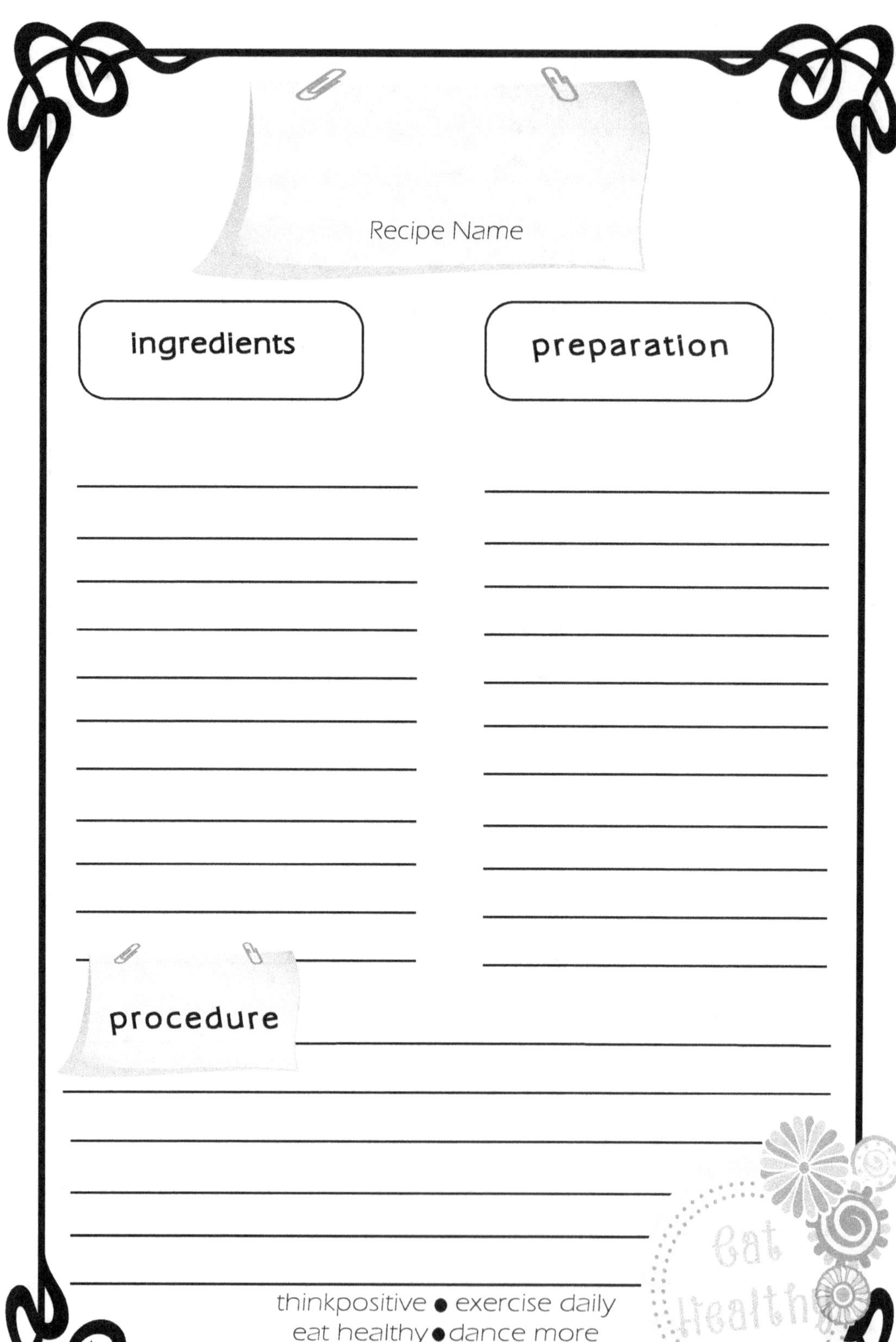
Recipe Name

ingredients

preparation

procedure

thinkpositive ● exercise daily
eat healthy ● dance more
Love often ● be happy

eat Healthy

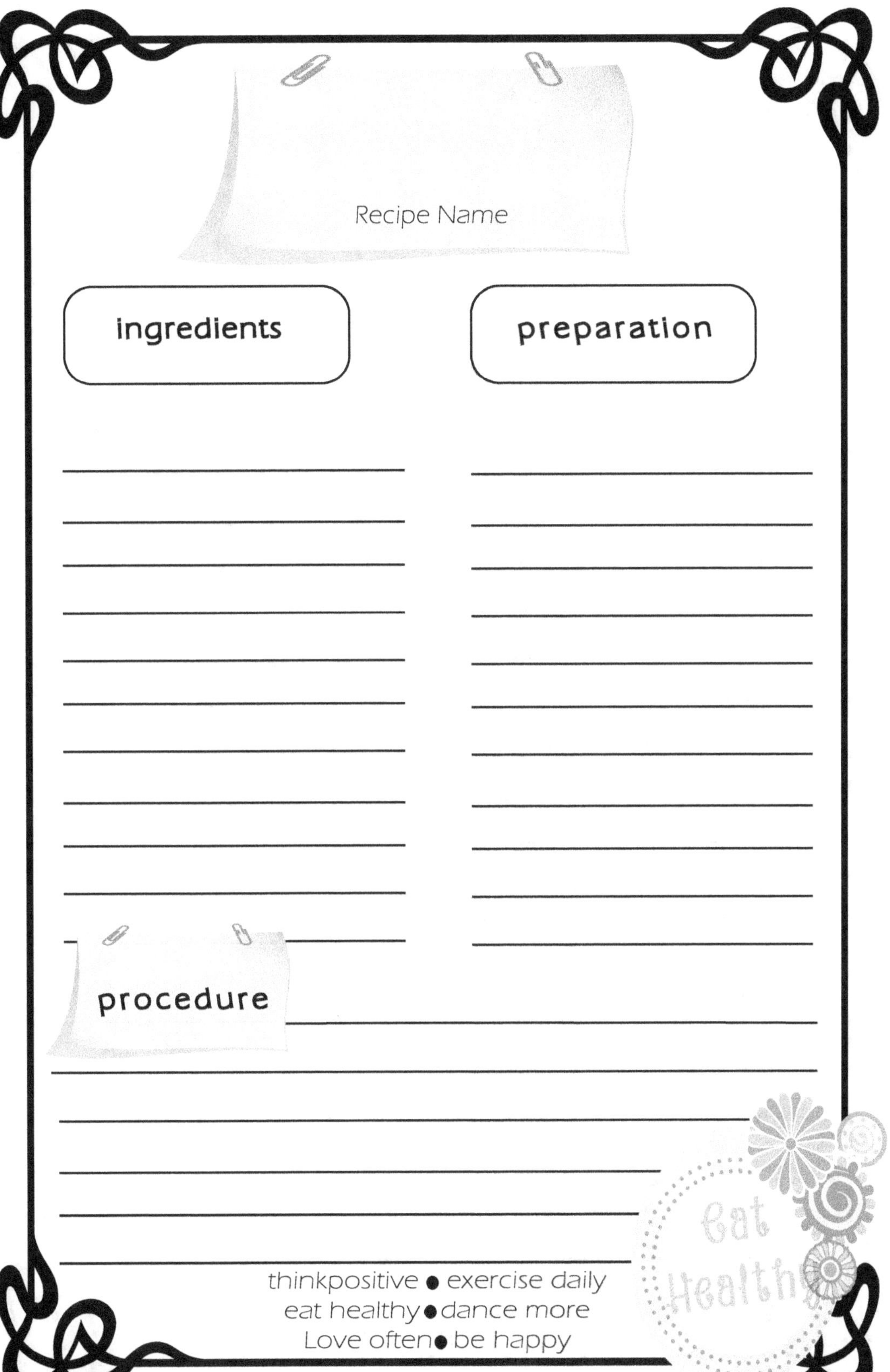

Recipe Name

ingredients

preparation

procedure

Recipe Name

ingredients

preparation

procedure

thinkpositive ● exercise daily
eat healthy ● dance more
Love often ● be happy

eat
Healthy

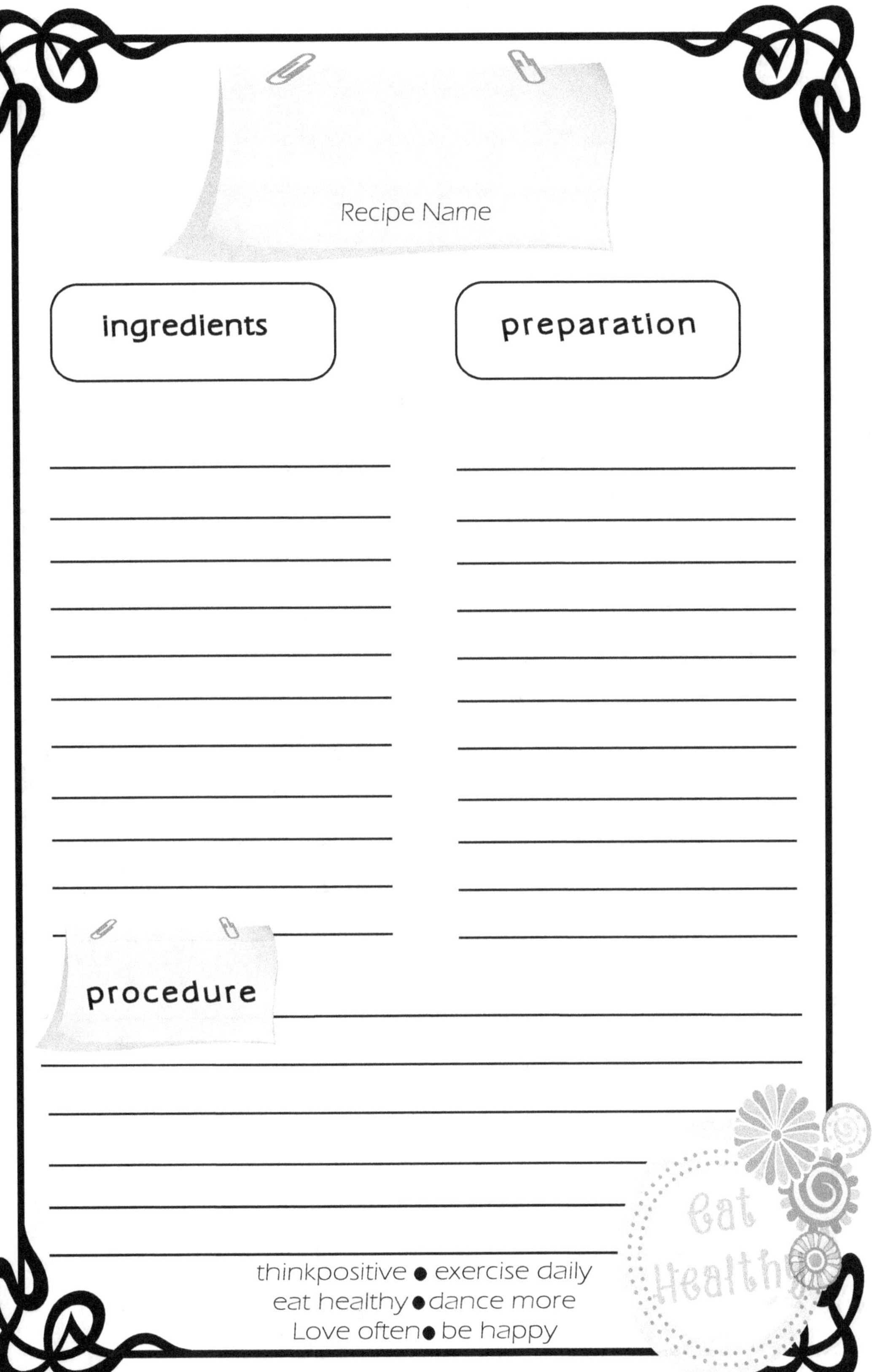

Recipe Name
ingredients
preparation
procedure
thinkpositive ● exercise daily
eat healthy ● dance more
Love often ● be happy
eat Healthy

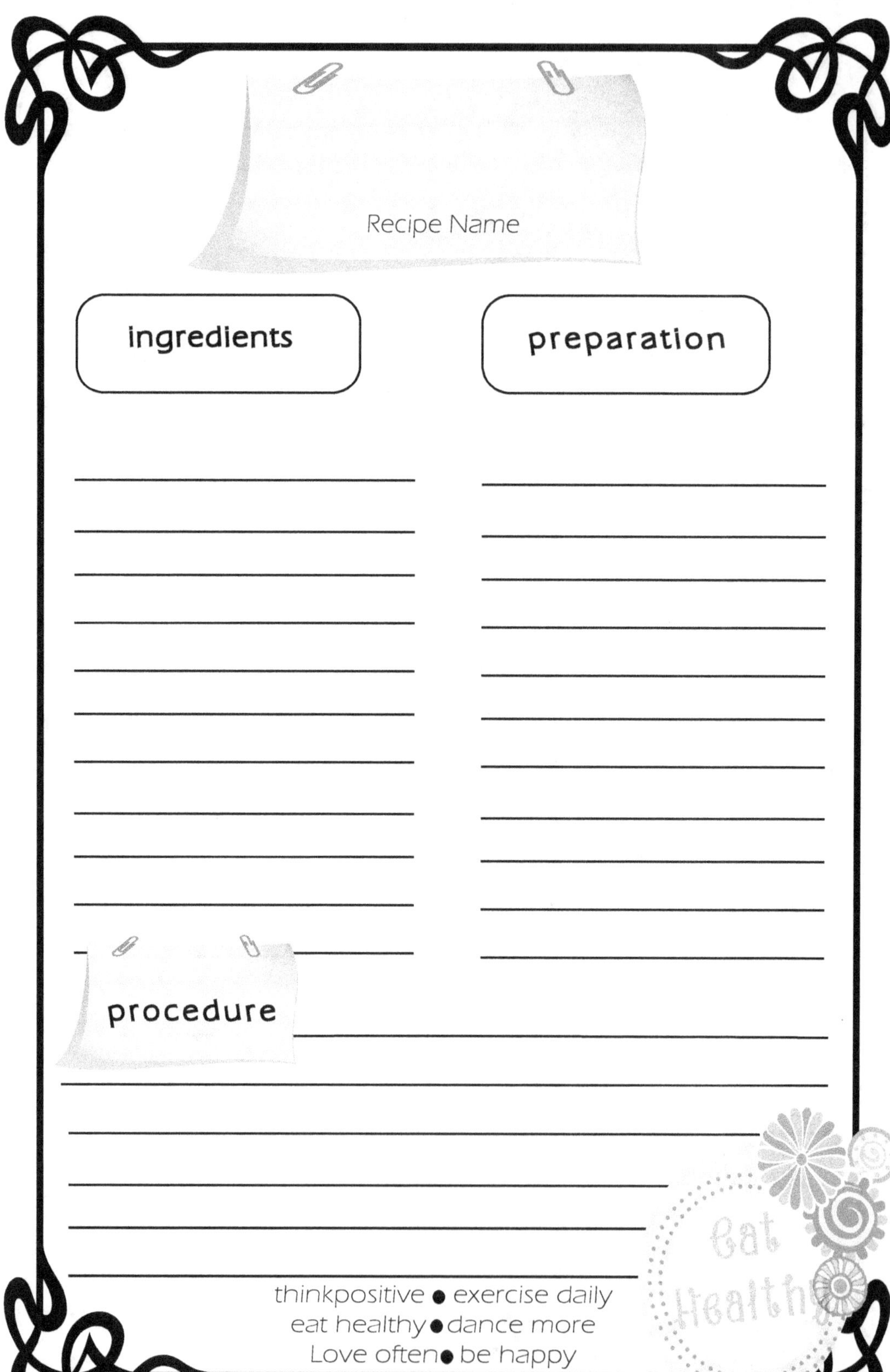

Recipe Name
ingredients
preparation
procedure
thinkpositive ● exercise daily
eat healthy ● dance more
Love often ● be happy
Eat Healthy

Recipe Name

ingredients

preparation

procedure

thinkpositive ● exercise daily
eat healthy ● dance more
Love often ● be happy

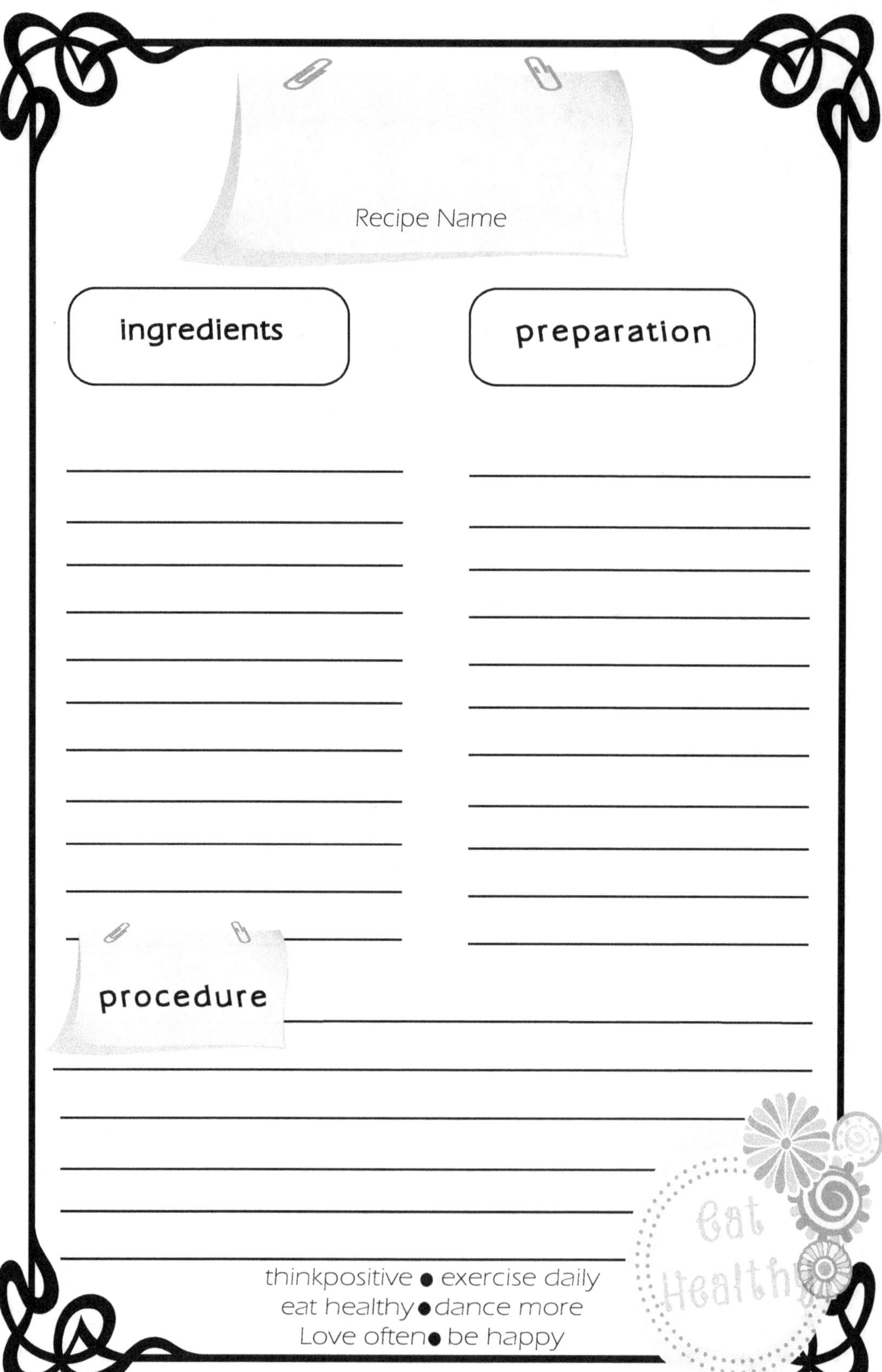

Recipe Name
ingredients
preparation
procedure
thinkpositive ● exercise daily
eat healthy ● dance more
Love often ● be happy
Eat Healthy

Recipe Name

ingredients

preparation

procedure

thinkpositive ● exercise daily
eat healthy ● dance more
Love often ● be happy

Recipe Name
ingredients
preparation
procedure
thinkpositive ● exercise daily
eat healthy ● dance more
Love often ● be happy
Eat Healthy

Recipe Name

ingredients

preparation

procedure

thinkpositive ● exercise daily
eat healthy ● dance more
Love often ● be happy

Eat Healthy

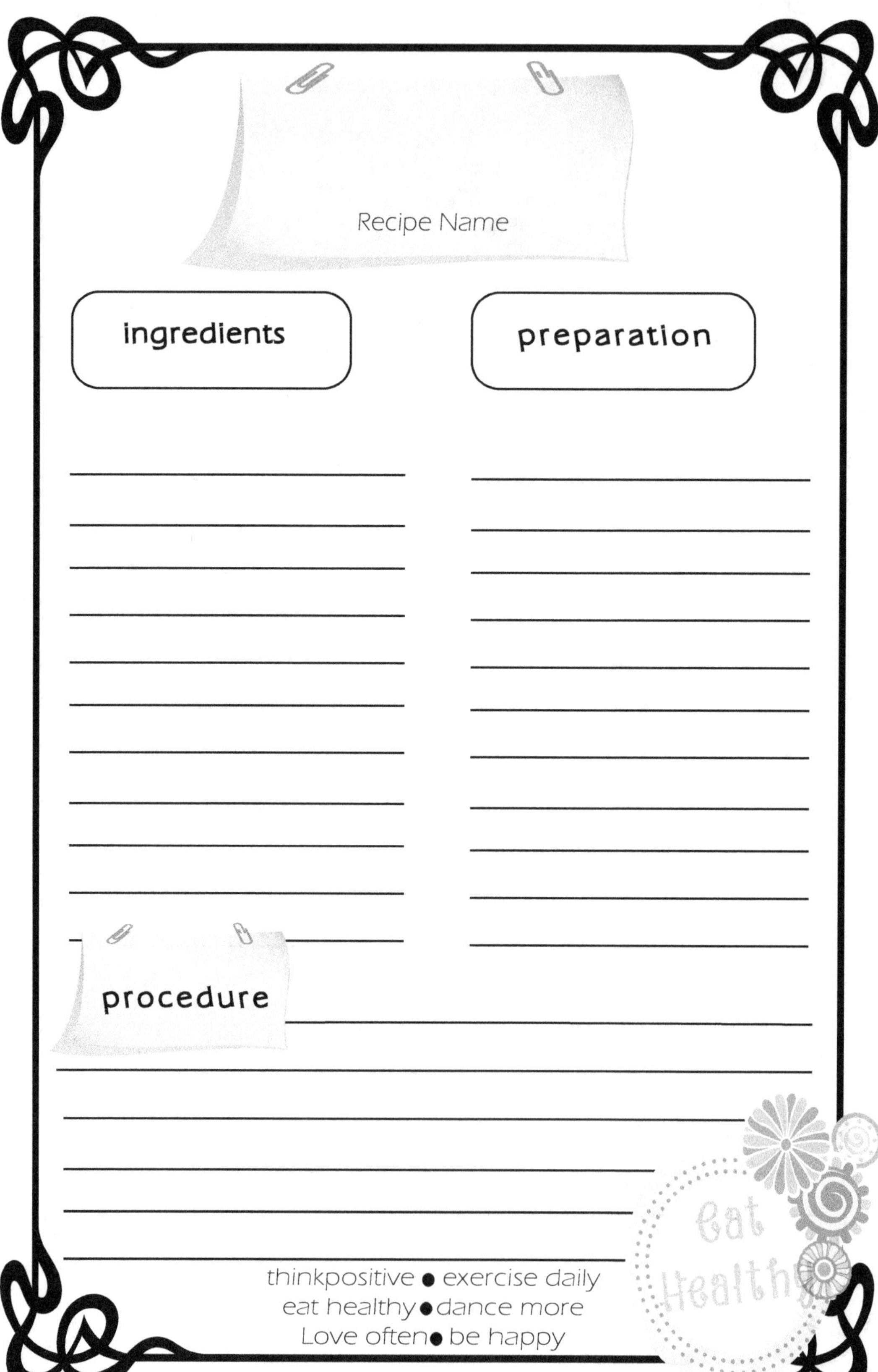

Recipe Name
ingredients
preparation
procedure
thinkpositive ● exercise daily
eat healthy ● dance more
Love often ● be happy
eat Healthy

Recipe Name

ingredients

preparation

procedure

thinkpositive ● exercise daily
eat healthy ● dance more
Love often ● be happy

Eat Healthy

Recipe Name

ingredients

preparation

procedure

thinkpositive ● exercise daily
eat healthy ● dance more
Love often ● be happy

Eat Healthy

Recipe Name

ingredients

preparation

procedure

Recipe Name

ingredients

preparation

procedure

thinkpositive ● exercise daily
eat healthy ● dance more
Love often ● be happy

eat Healthy

Recipe Name

ingredients

preparation

procedure

thinkpositive ● exercise daily
eat healthy ● dance more
Love often ● be happy

Eat Healthy

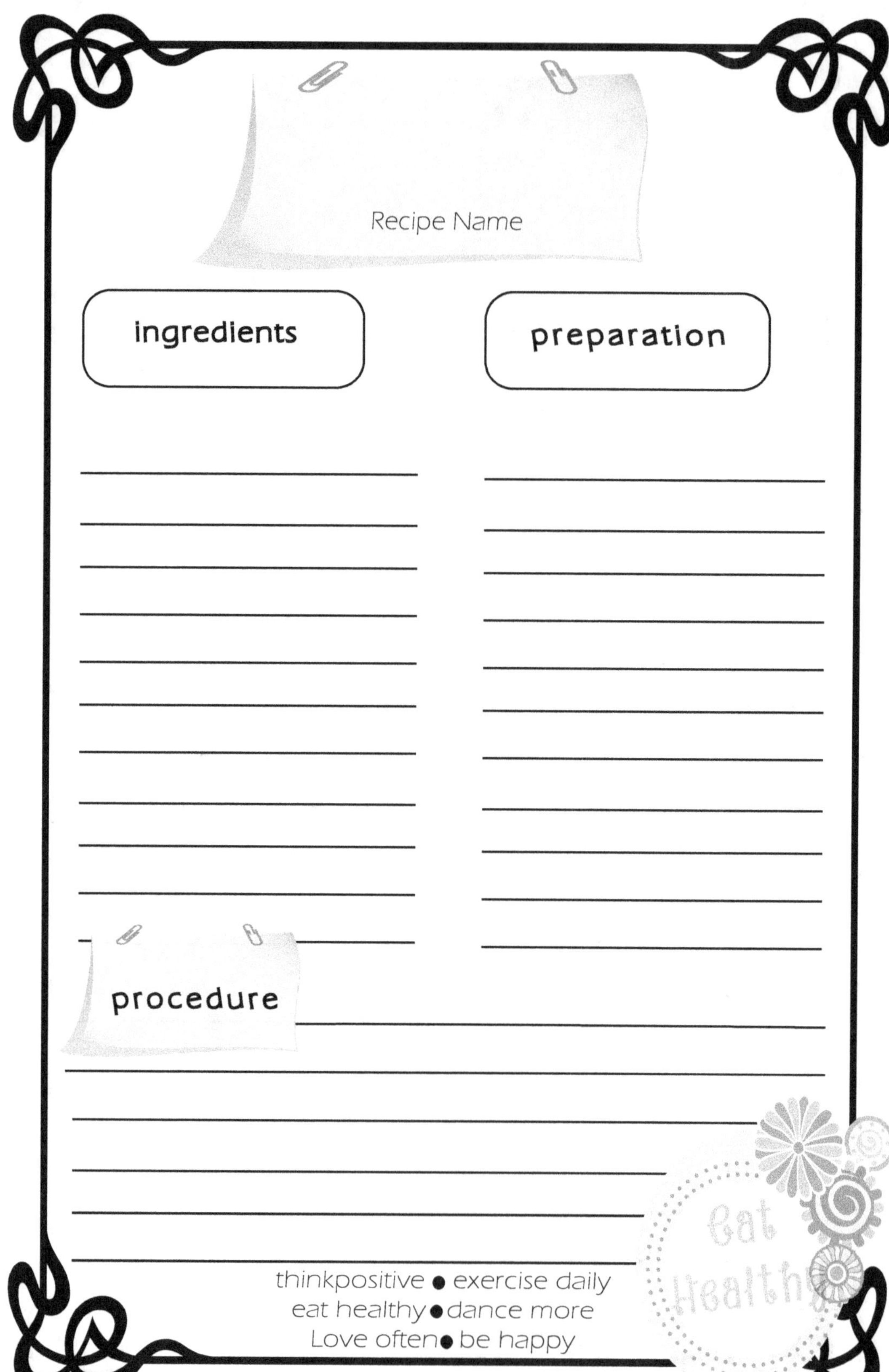
Recipe Name
ingredients
preparation
procedure
thinkpositive ● exercise daily
eat healthy ● dance more
Love often ● be happy
Eat Healthy

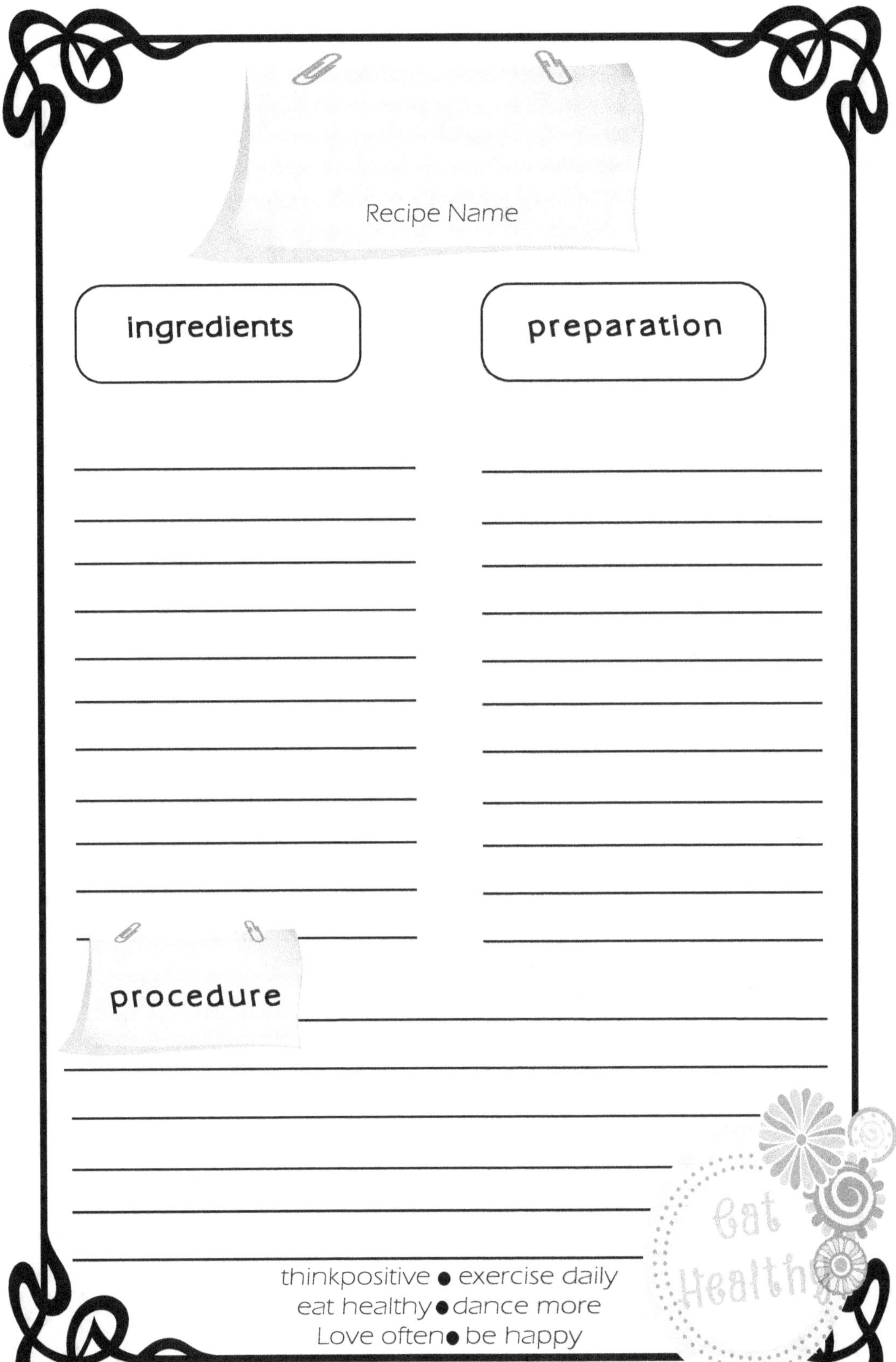

Recipe Name
ingredients
preparation
procedure
thinkpositive ● exercise daily
eat healthy ● dance more
Love often ● be happy
Eat Healthy

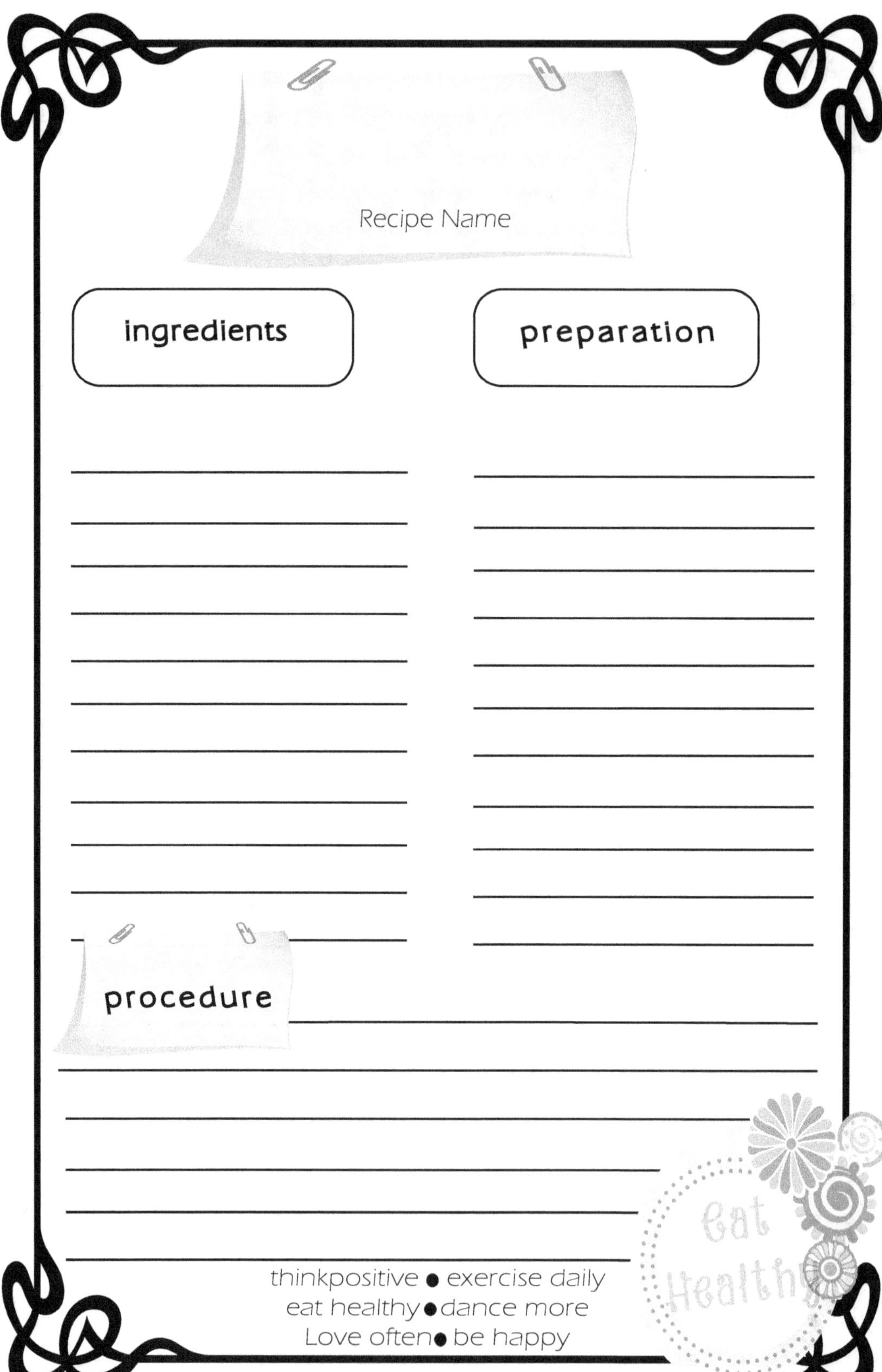

Recipe Name

ingredients

preparation

procedure

thinkpositive ● exercise daily
eat healthy ● dance more
Love often ● be happy

Eat Healthy

Recipe Name

ingredients

preparation

procedure

thinkpositive ● exercise daily
eat healthy ● dance more
Love often ● be happy

Eat Healthy

Recipe Name

ingredients

preparation

procedure

thinkpositive ● exercise daily
eat healthy ● dance more
Love often ● be happy

Eat Healthy

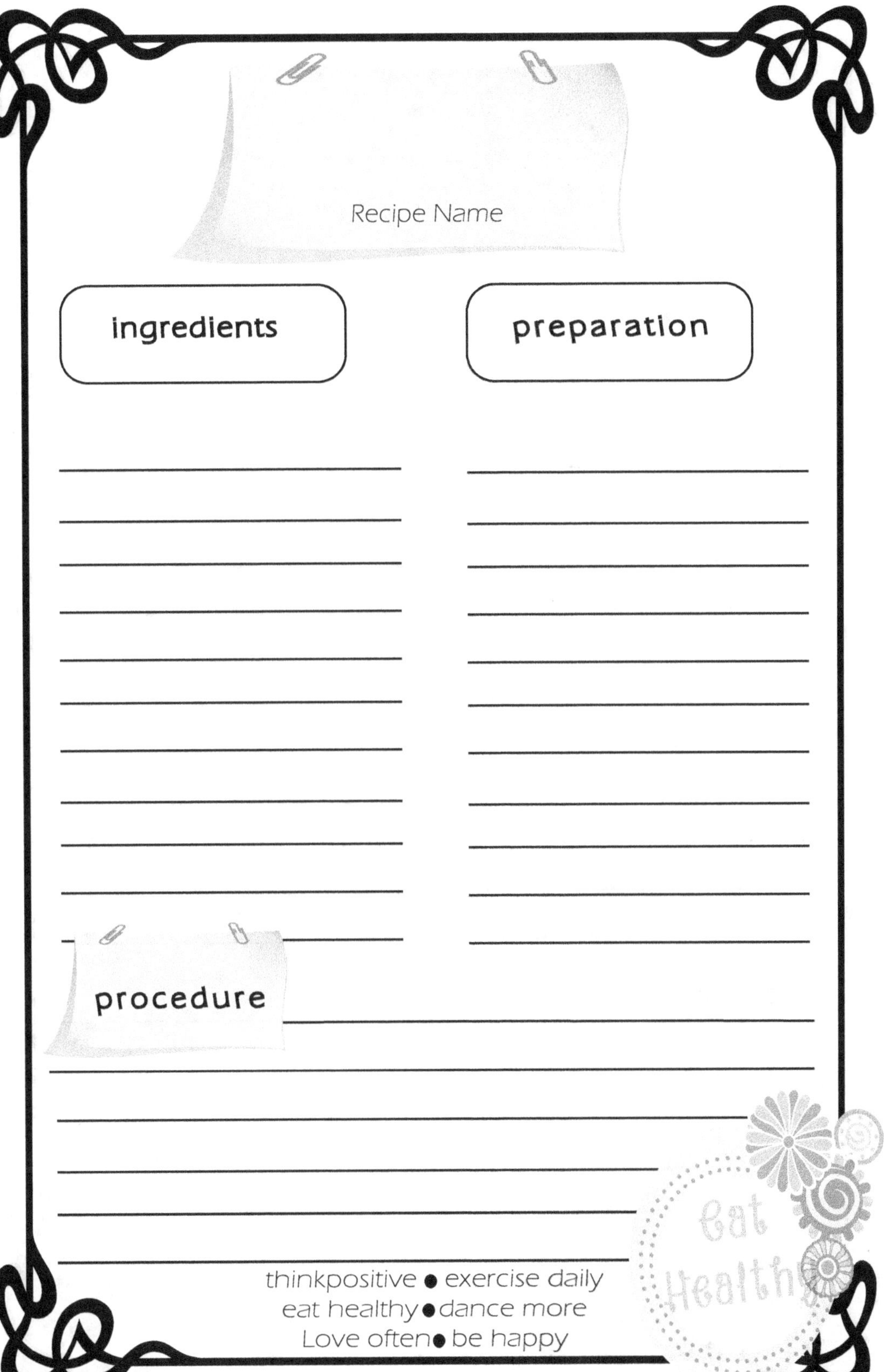

Recipe Name

ingredients

preparation

procedure

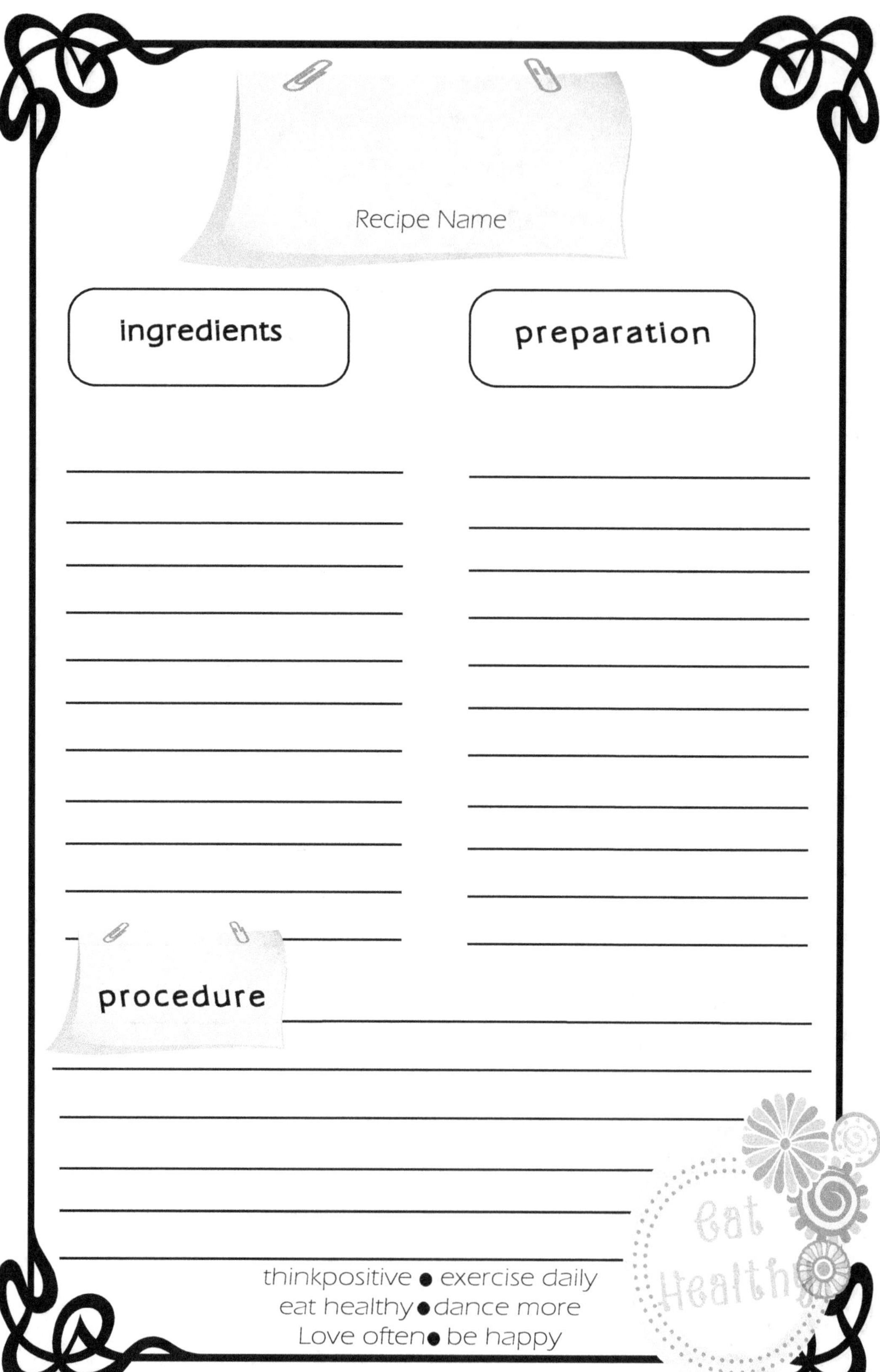

Recipe Name
ingredients
preparation
procedure
thinkpositive ● exercise daily
eat healthy ● dance more
Love often ● be happy
Eat Healthy

Recipe Name

ingredients

preparation

procedure

thinkpositive ● exercise daily
eat healthy ● dance more
Love often ● be happy

Eat Healthy

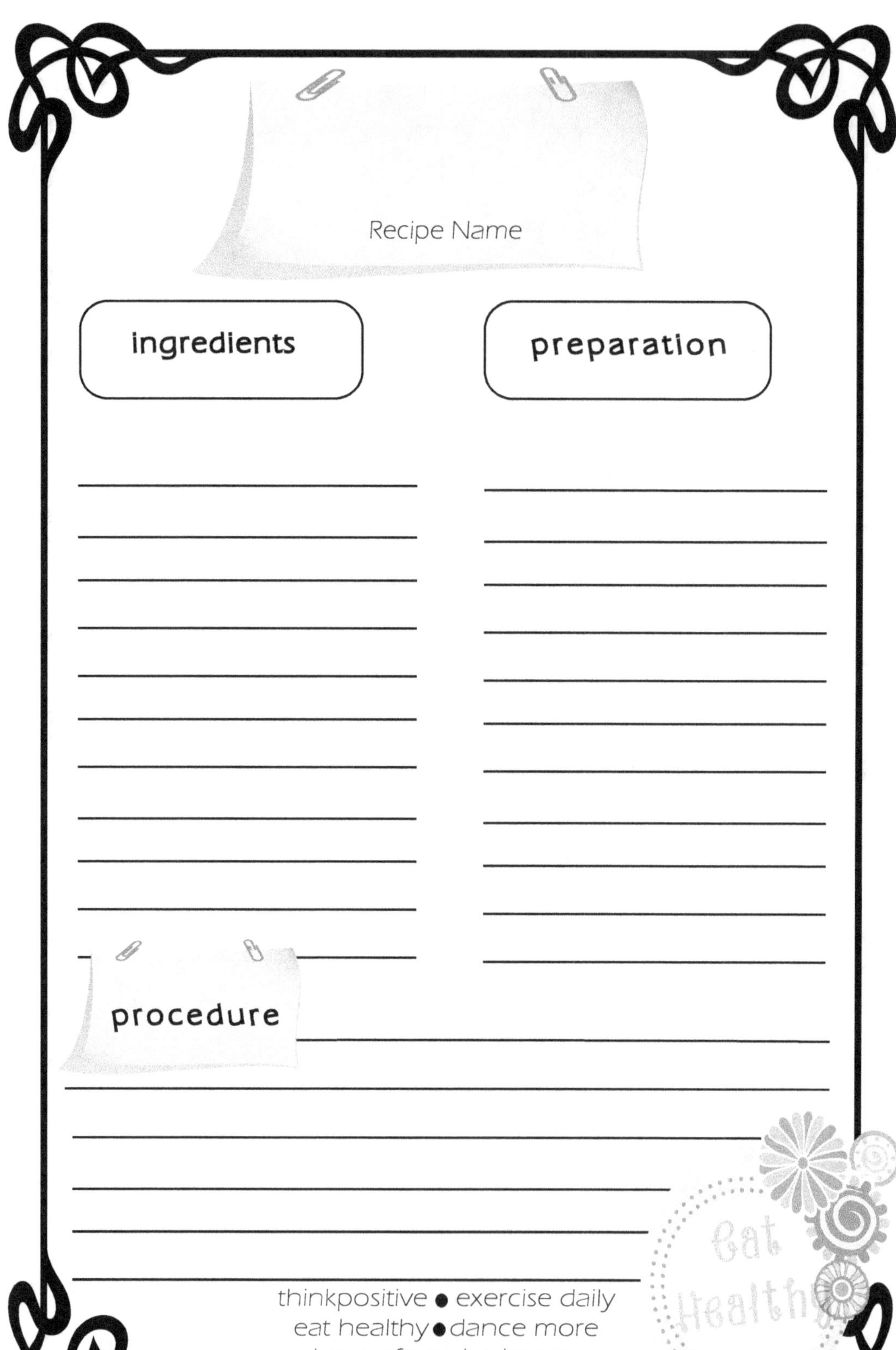

Recipe Name

ingredients

preparation

procedure

thinkpositive ● exercise daily
eat healthy ● dance more
Love often ● be happy

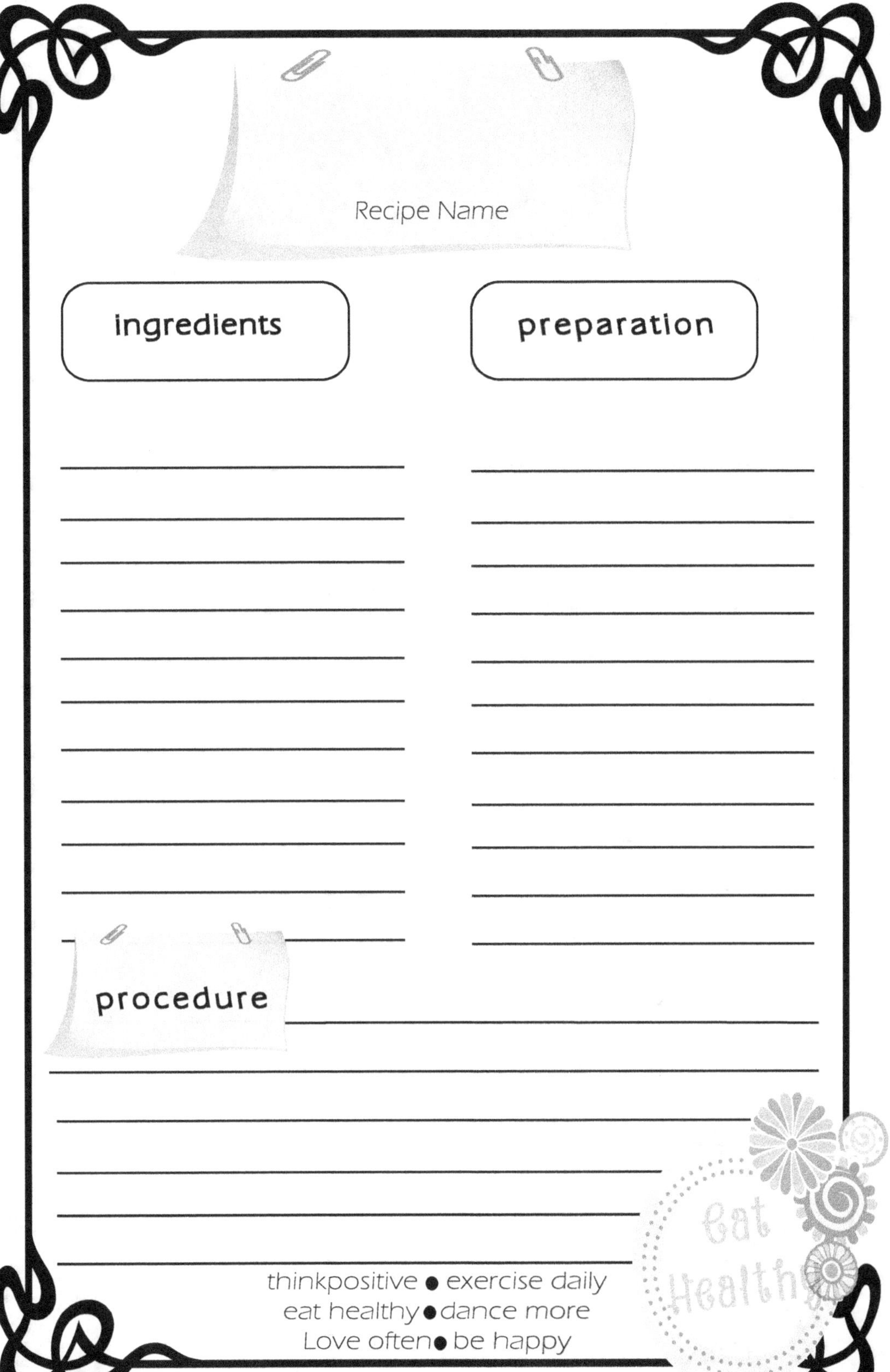

Recipe Name

ingredients

preparation

procedure

thinkpositive ● exercise daily
eat healthy ● dance more
Love often ● be happy

Eat Healthy

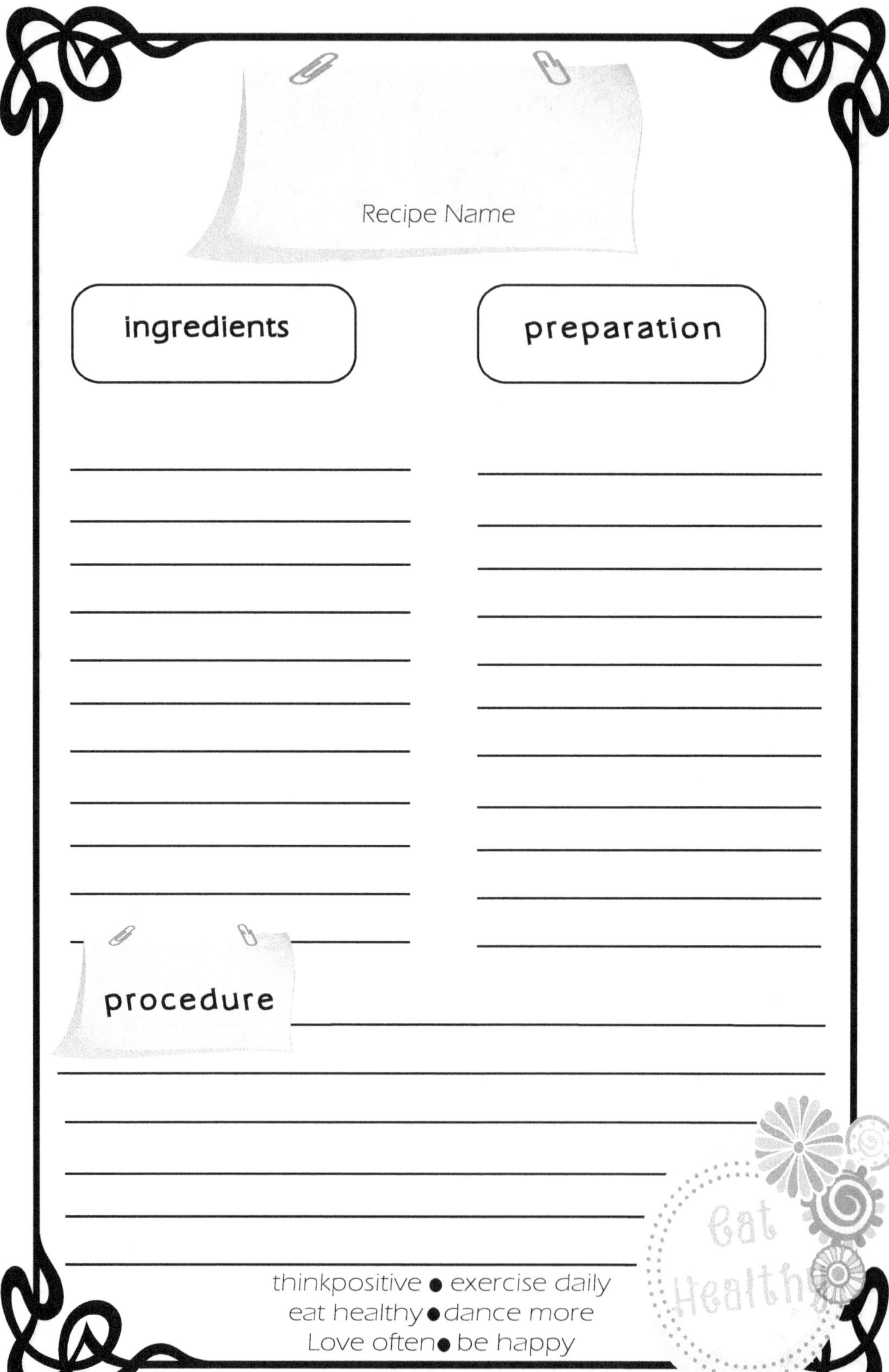

Recipe Name

ingredients

preparation

procedure

thinkpositive ● exercise daily
eat healthy ● dance more
Love often ● be happy

Eat Healthy

Recipe Name

ingredients

preparation

procedure

thinkpositive ● exercise daily
eat healthy ● dance more
Love often ● be happy

Eat
Healthy

Recipe Name

ingredients

preparation

procedure

thinkpositive ● exercise daily
eat healthy ● dance more
Love often ● be happy

Eat Healthy

Recipe Name

ingredients

preparation

procedure

thinkpositive ● exercise daily
eat healthy ● dance more
Love often ● be happy

Eat Healthy

Recipe Name
ingredients
preparation
procedure
thinkpositive ● exercise daily
eat healthy ● dance more
Love often ● be happy
Eat Healthy

Recipe Name
ingredients
preparation
procedure
thinkpositive ● exercise daily
eat healthy ● dance more
Love often ● be happy
Eat Healthy

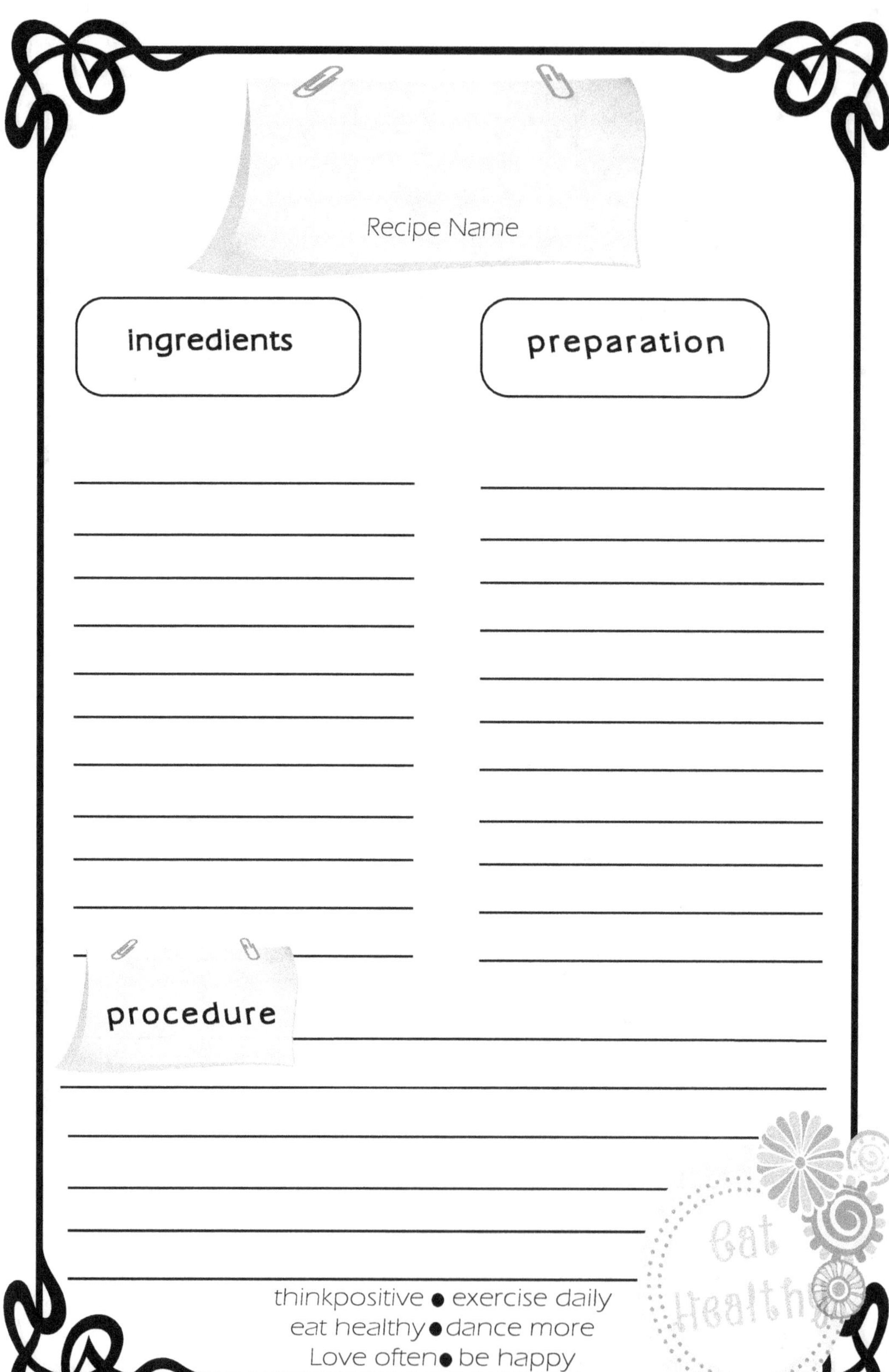

Recipe Name

ingredients

preparation

procedure

Recipe Name

ingredients

preparation

procedure

thinkpositive ● exercise daily
eat healthy ● dance more
Love often ● be happy

Eat Healthy

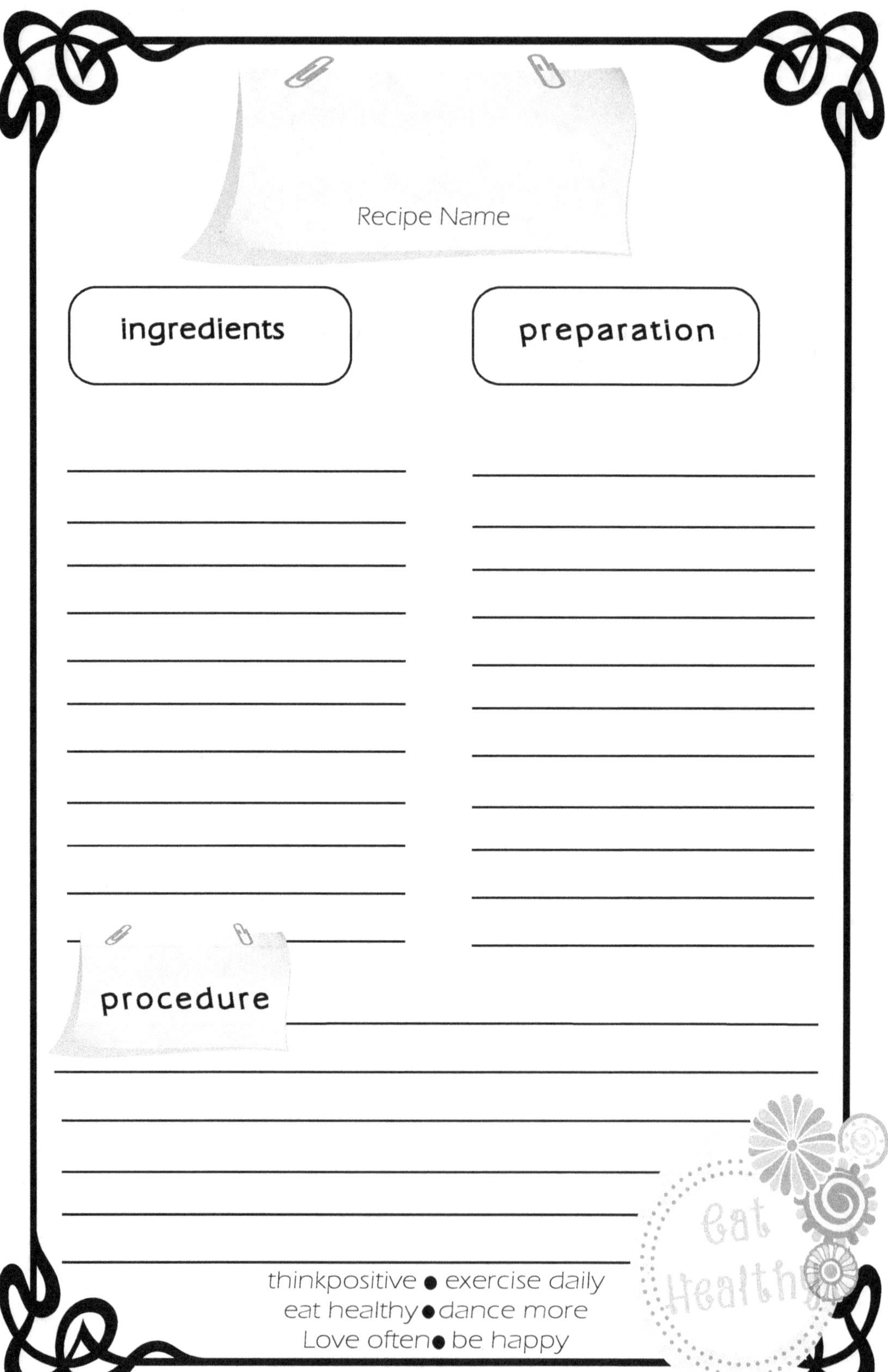

Recipe Name
ingredients
preparation
procedure
thinkpositive ● exercise daily
eat healthy ● dance more
Love often ● be happy
Eat Healthy

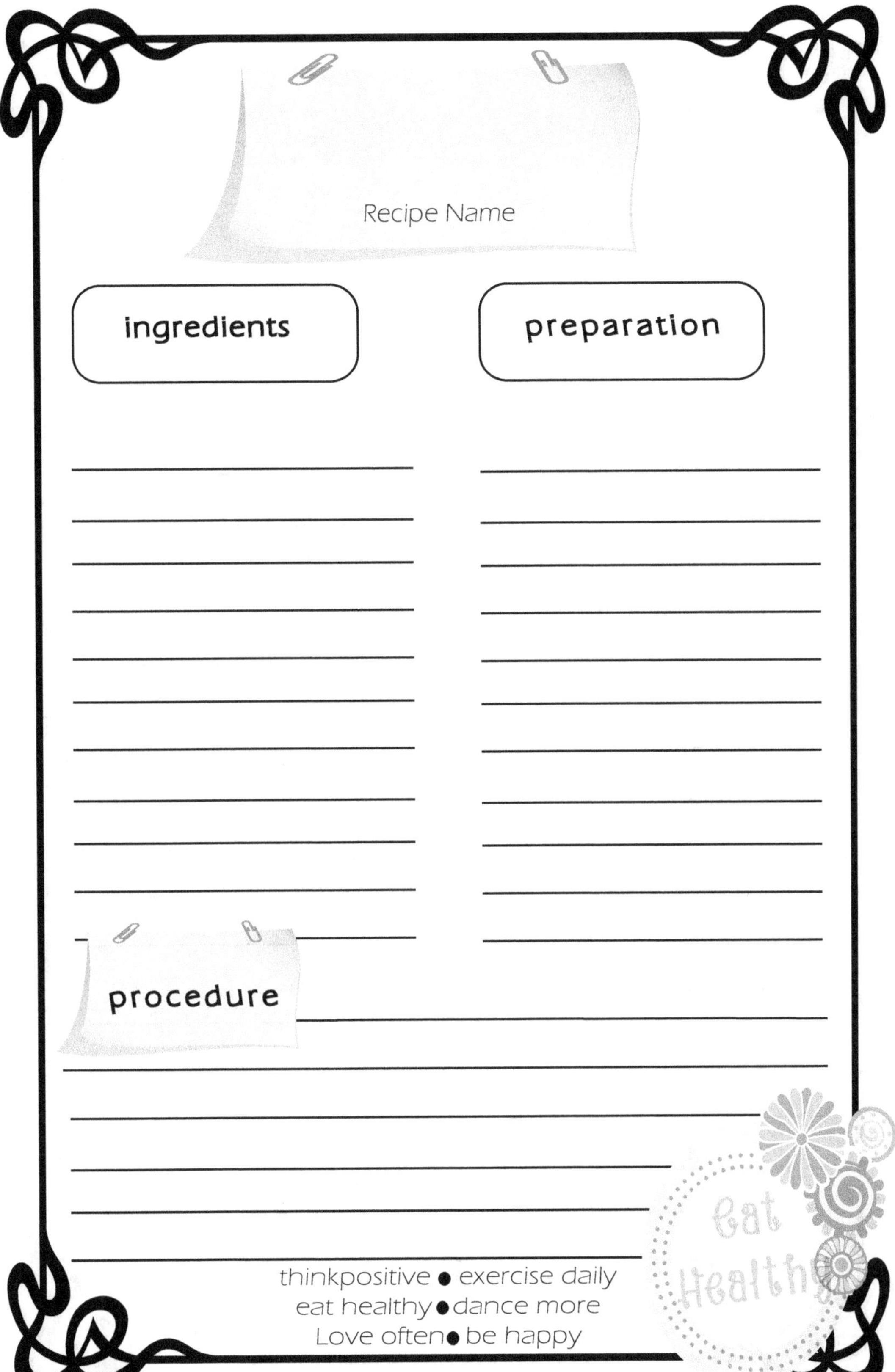

Recipe Name

ingredients

preparation

procedure

thinkpositive ● exercise daily
eat healthy ● dance more
Love often ● be happy

Eat
Healthy

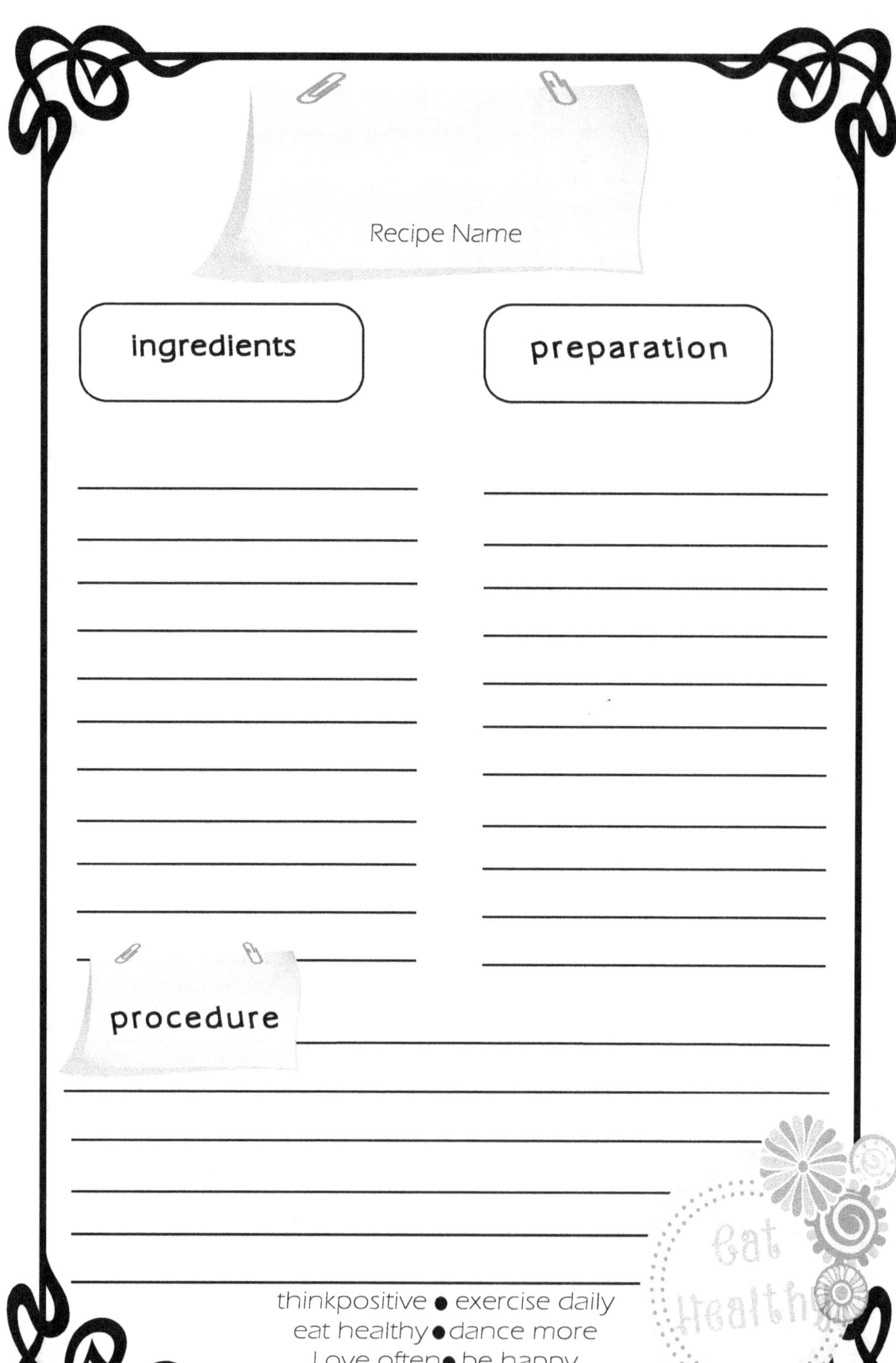
Recipe Name

ingredients

preparation

procedure

thinkpositive ● exercise daily
eat healthy ● dance more
Love often ● be happy

Eat Healthy

Recipe Name

ingredients

preparation

procedure

thinkpositive ● exercise daily
eat healthy ● dance more
Love often ● be happy

Eat Healthy

Recipe Name

ingredients

preparation

procedure

thinkpositive ● exercise daily
eat healthy ● dance more
Love often ● be happy

Eat Healthy

Recipe Name
ingredients
preparation
procedure
thinkpositive ● exercise daily
eat healthy ● dance more
Love often ● be happy
Eat Healthy

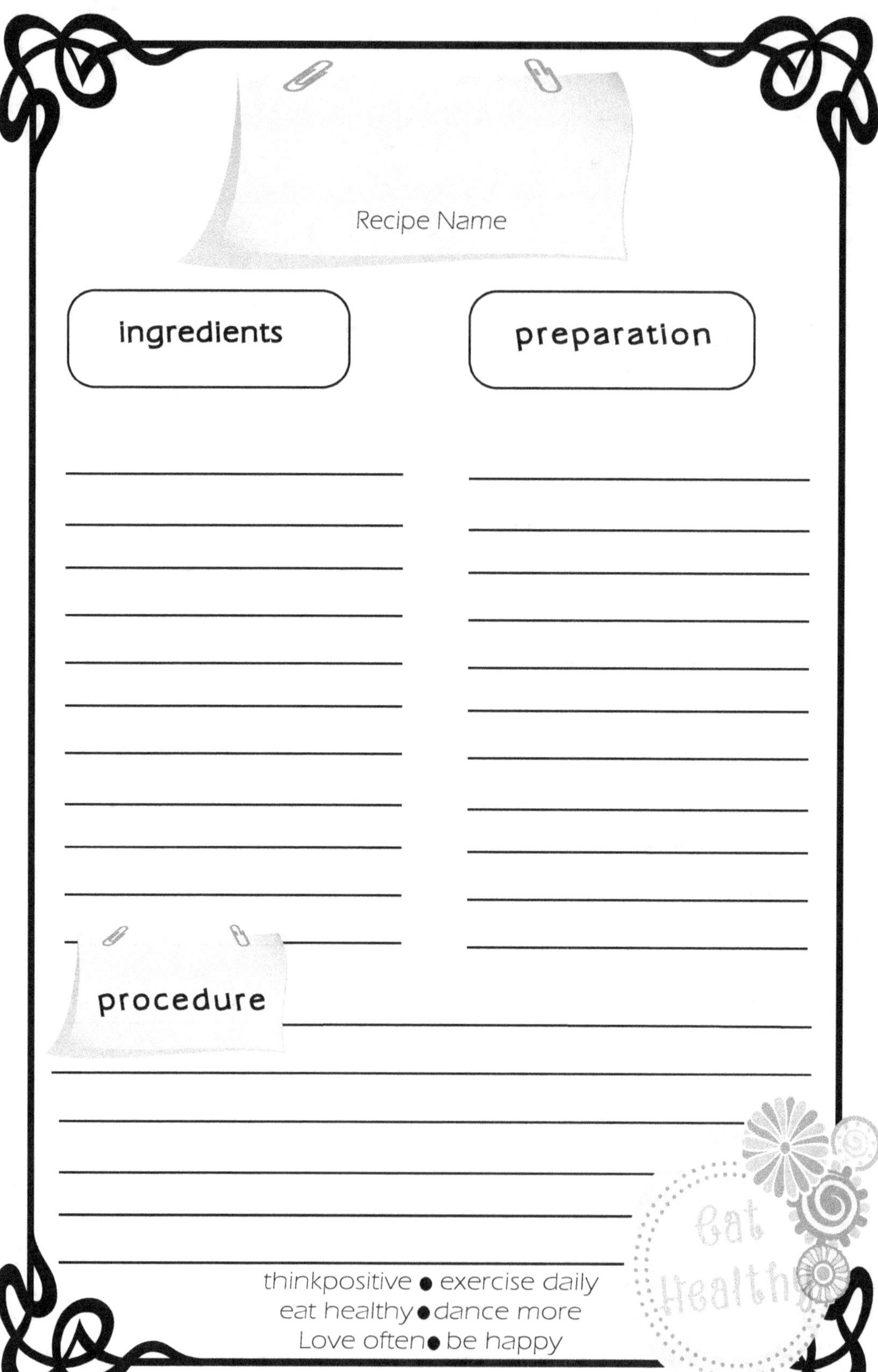

Recipe Name

ingredients

preparation

procedure

thinkpositive ● exercise daily
eat healthy ● dance more
Love often ● be happy

Eat Healthy

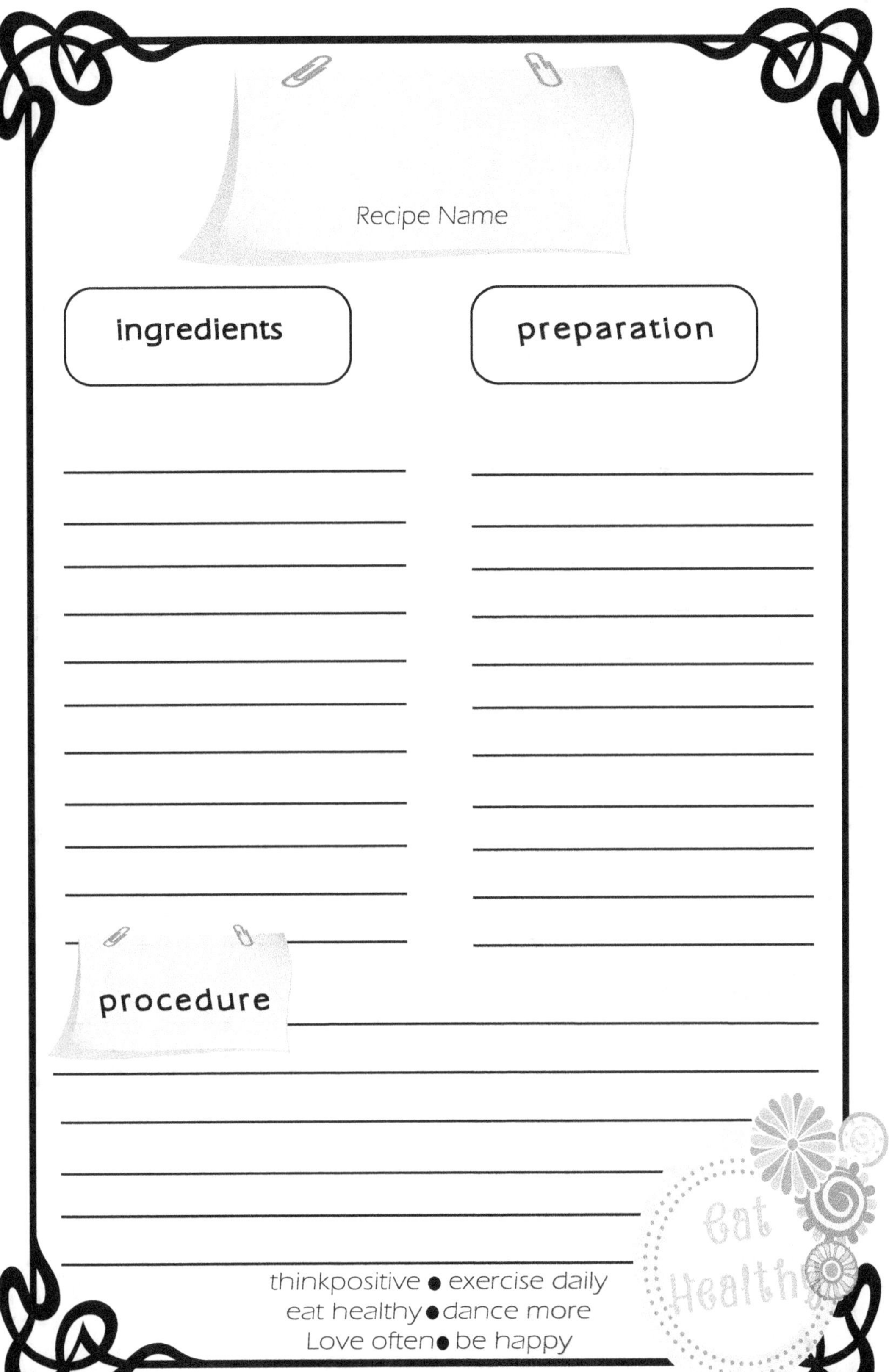

Recipe Name

ingredients

preparation

procedure

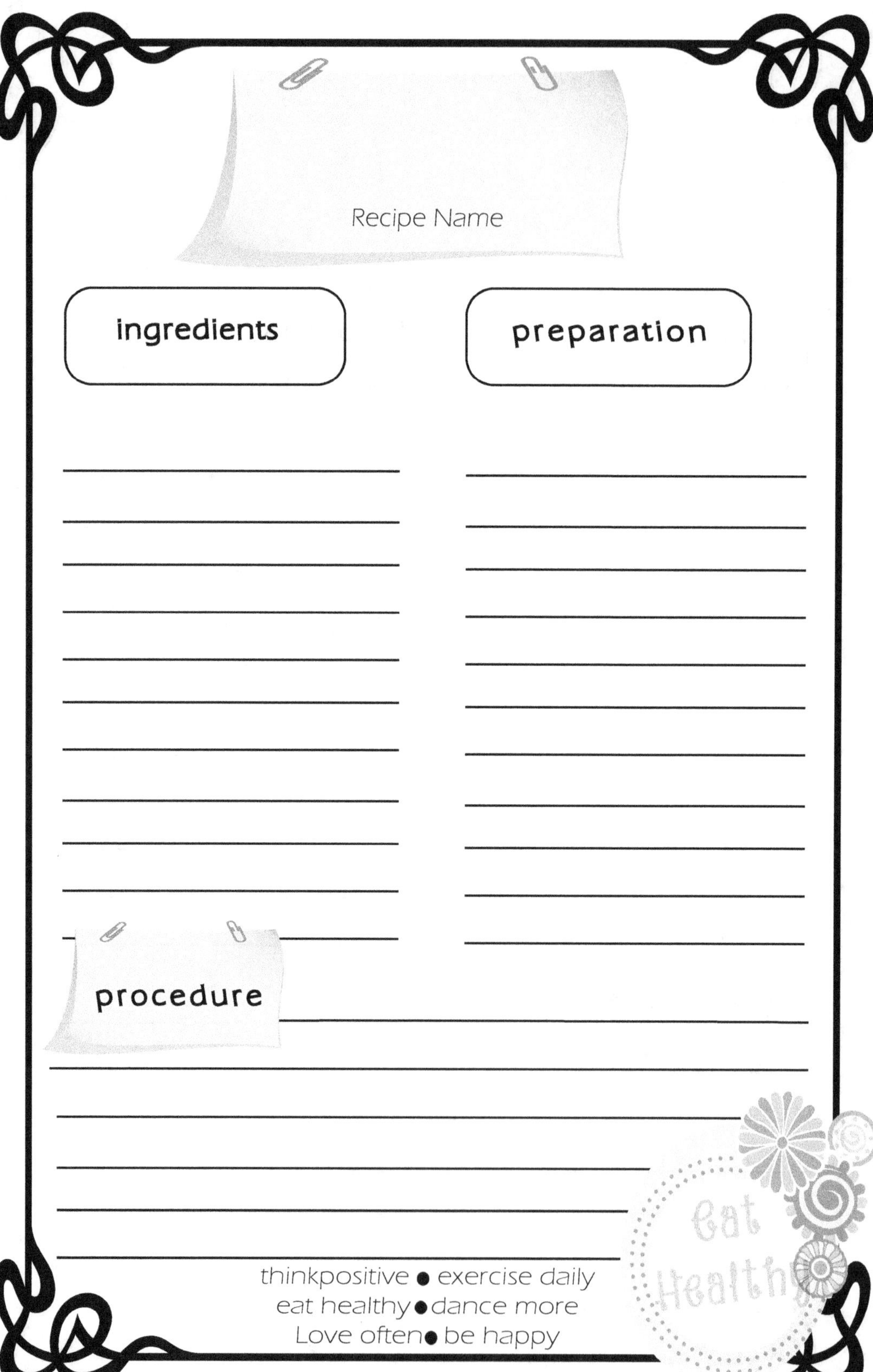

Recipe Name
ingredients
preparation
procedure
thinkpositive ● exercise daily
eat healthy ● dance more
Love often ● be happy
Eat Healthy

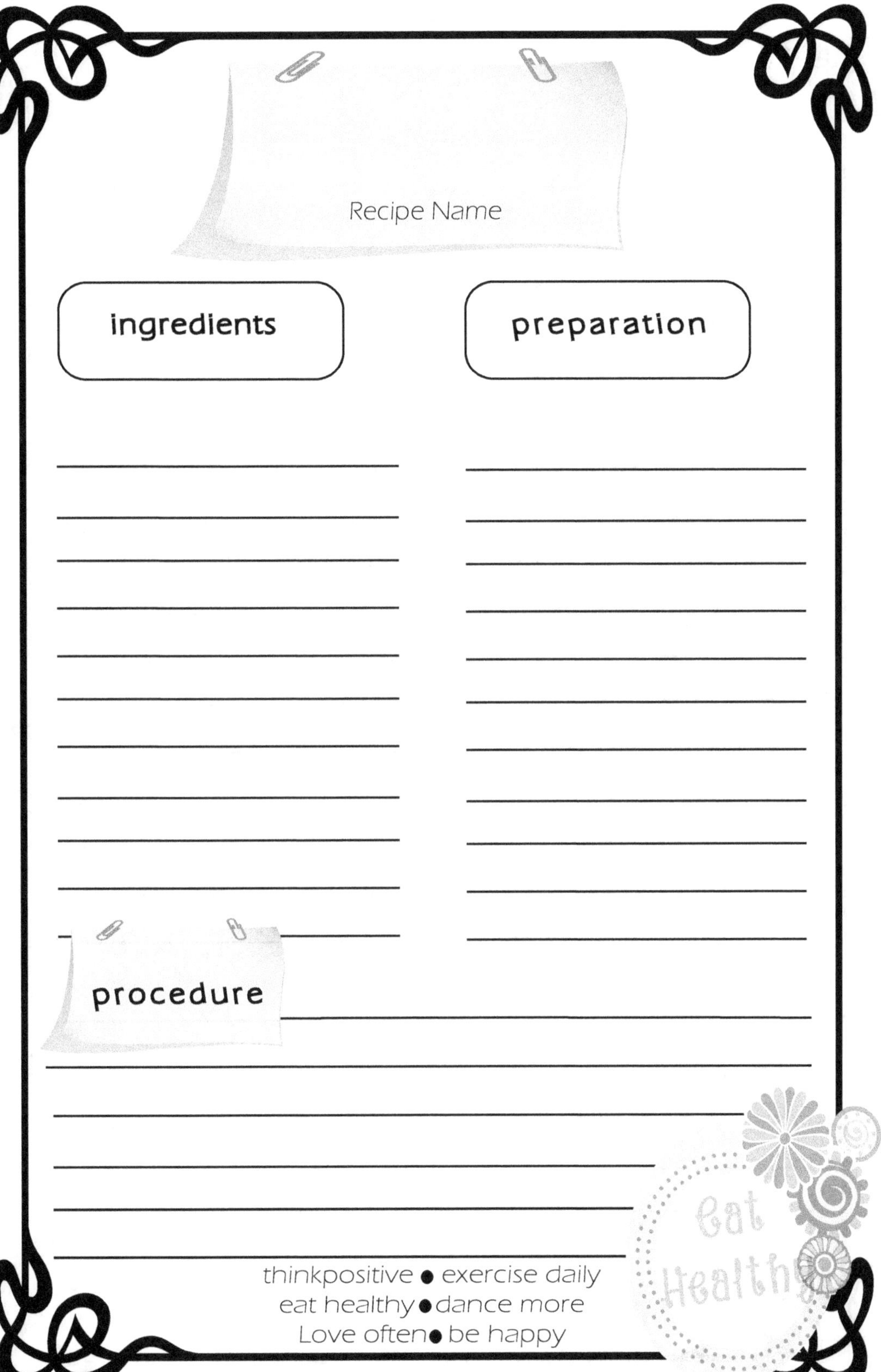
Recipe Name

ingredients

preparation

procedure

thinkpositive ● exercise daily
eat healthy ● dance more
Love often ● be happy

Eat Healthy

Recipe Name

ingredients

preparation

procedure

thinkpositive ● exercise daily
eat healthy ● dance more
Love often ● be happy

Eat Healthy

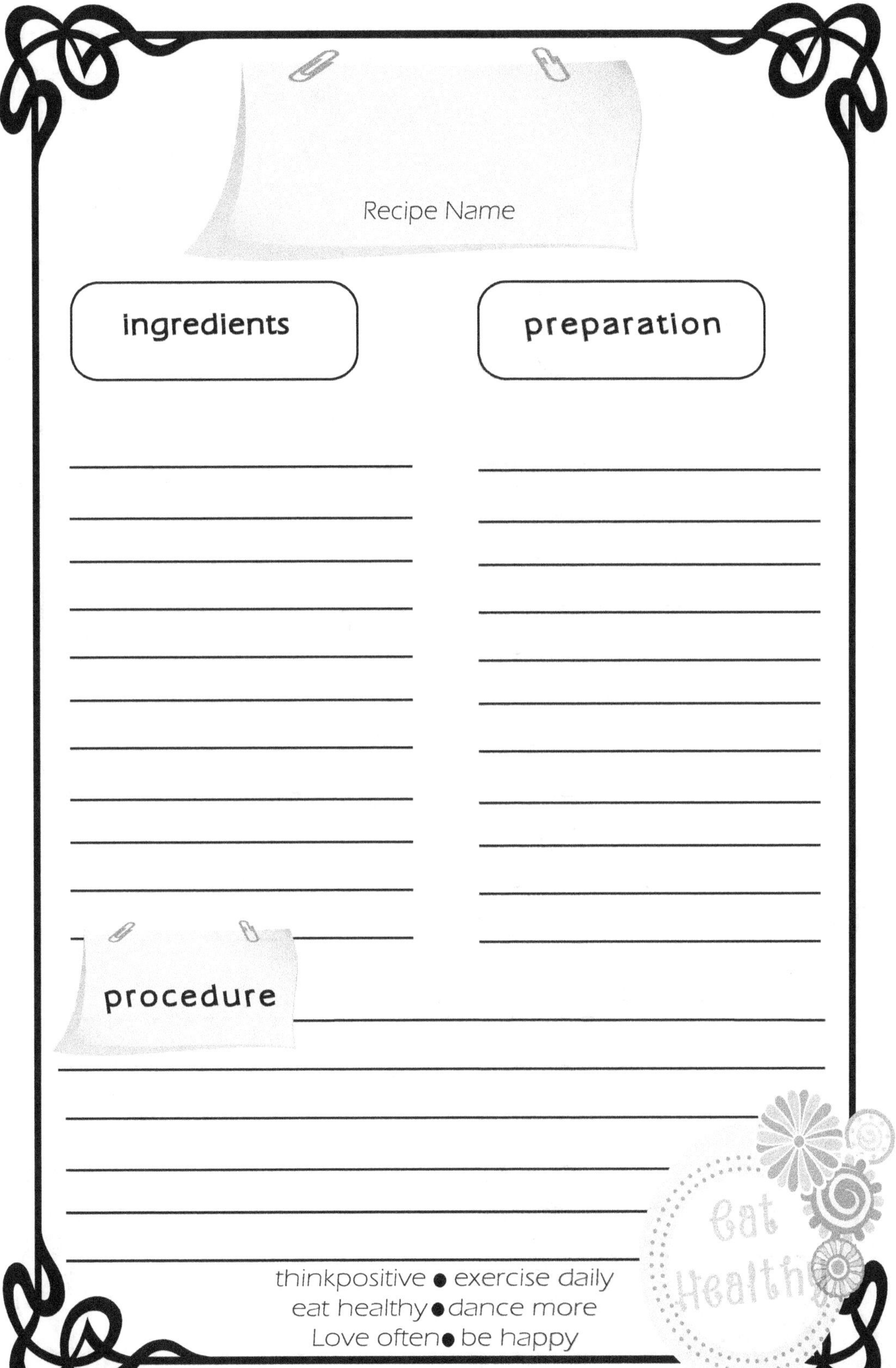

Recipe Name

ingredients

preparation

procedure

thinkpositive ● exercise daily
eat healthy ● dance more
Love often ● be happy

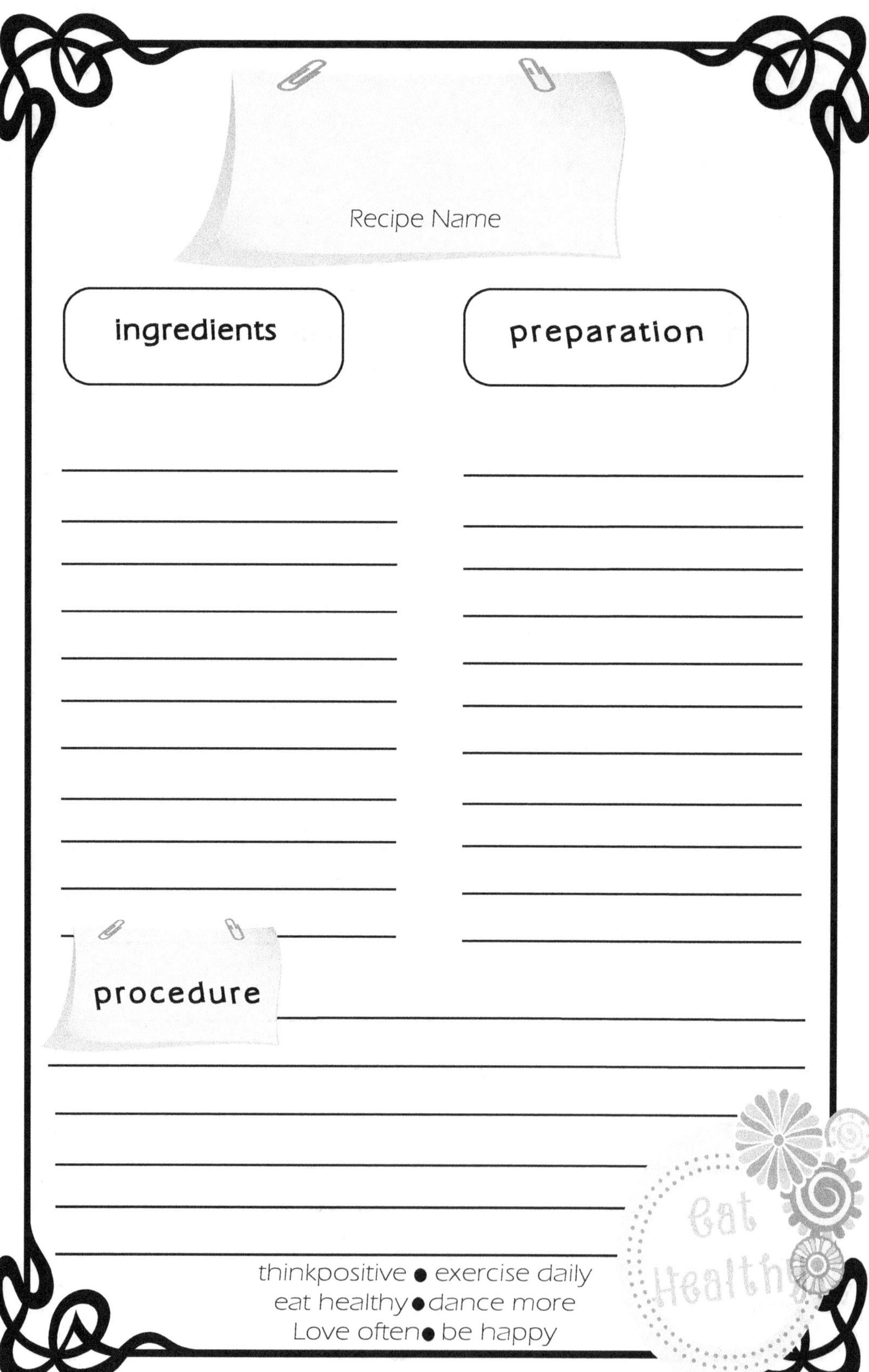

Recipe Name
ingredients
preparation
procedure
thinkpositive ● exercise daily
eat healthy ● dance more
Love often ● be happy
Eat Healthy

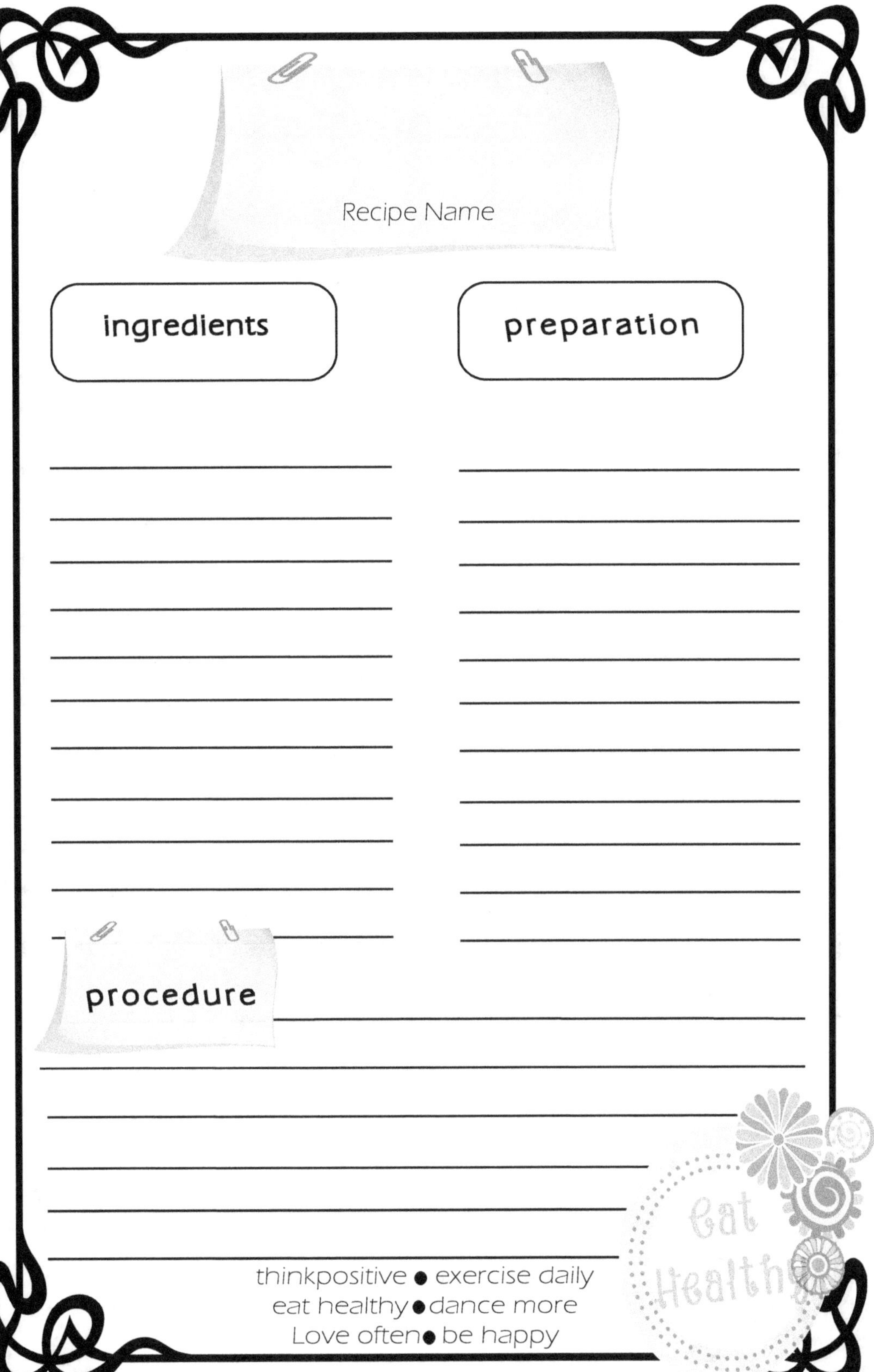

Recipe Name

ingredients

preparation

procedure

thinkpositive ● exercise daily
eat healthy ● dance more
Love often ● be happy

eat Healthy

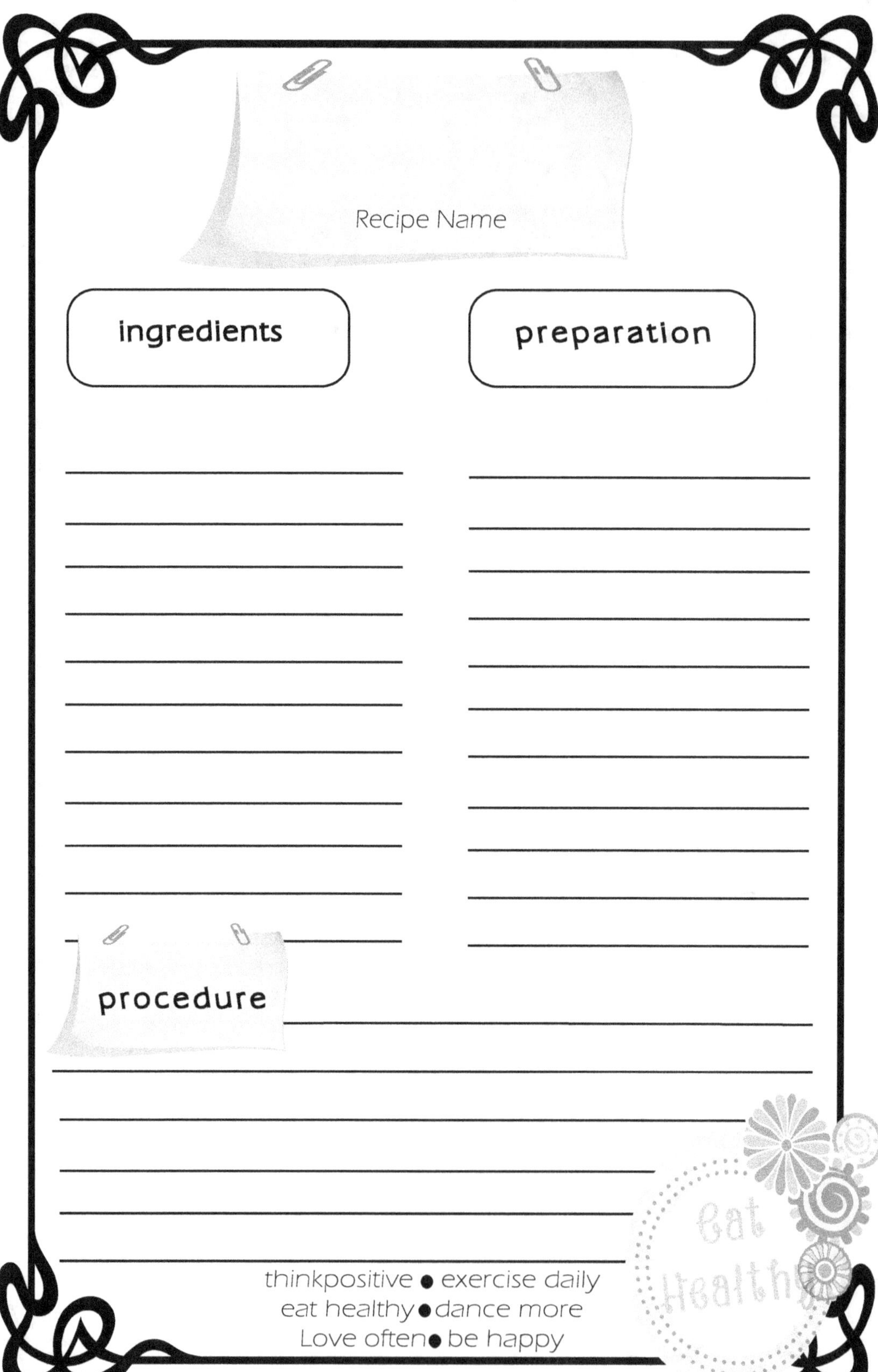

Recipe Name

ingredients

preparation

procedure

thinkpositive ● exercise daily
eat healthy ● dance more
Love often ● be happy

Eat Healthy

Recipe Name

ingredients

preparation

procedure

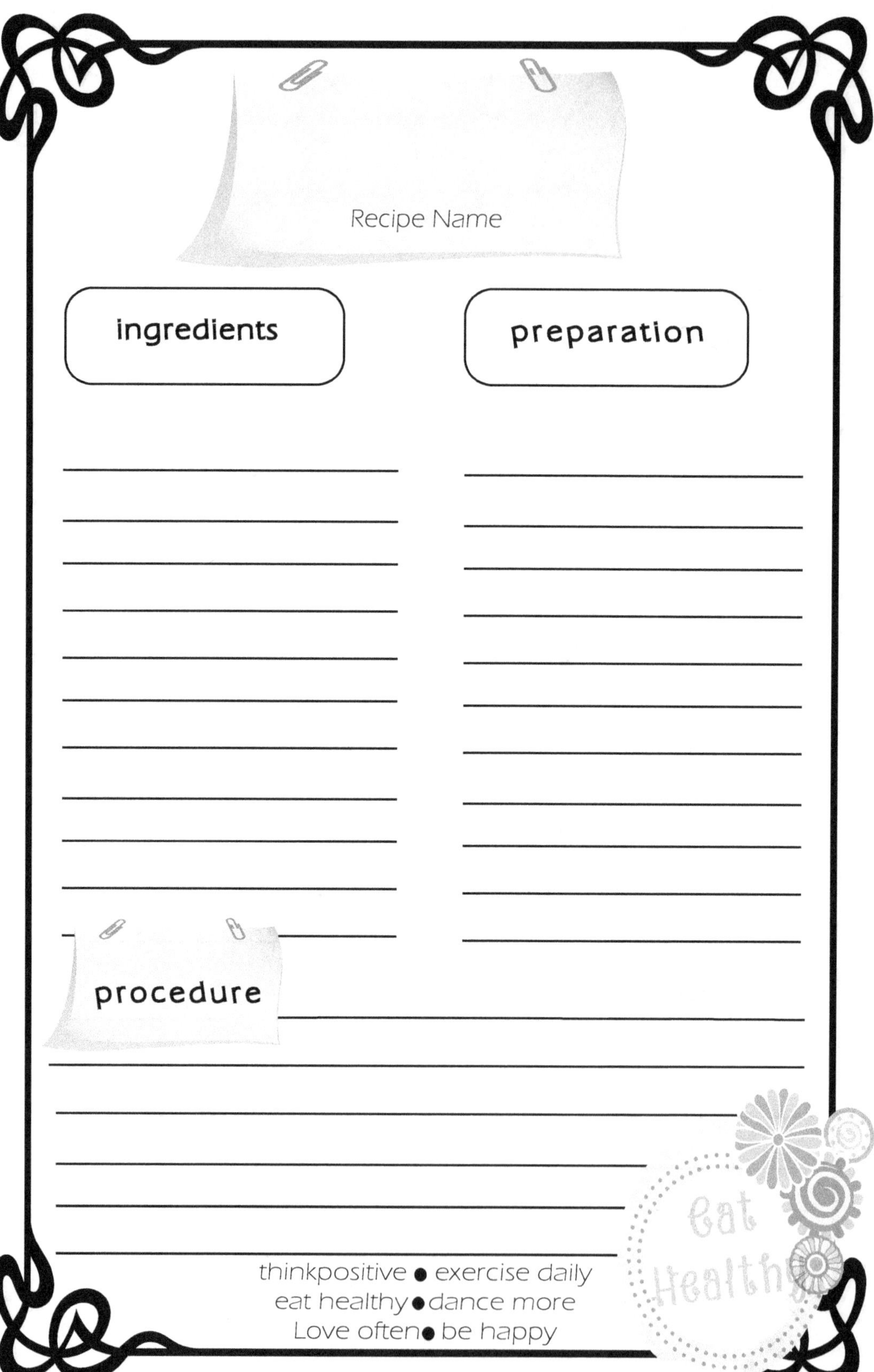

Recipe Name
ingredients
preparation
procedure
thinkpositive ● exercise daily
eat healthy ● dance more
Love often ● be happy
eat Healthy

Recipe Name

ingredients

preparation

procedure

thinkpositive ● exercise daily
eat healthy ● dance more
Love often ● be happy

www.ingramcontent.com/pod-product-compliance
Lightning Source LLC
Chambersburg PA
CBHW081311250726
48662CB00008B/2512